D0293933

The Industrial Revolution

Panorama of History Series
This series has been created to provide a vivid portrayal of major events in world history. Each text is concise but authoritative, giving essential facts combined with an insight into the character of the period and people involved. Every book includes a large number of full-colour illustrations and many more in black and white all researched from contemporary sources; these paintings, prints, maps and photographs all carry informative captions and are carefully integrated with the text. Other titles already published are **The Battle of Trafalgar, Last of the Tsars** and **The Spanish Armada.** Further 'Panoramas' will be added to the series at regular intervals.

Conditions of sale

This book shall not, by way of trade or otherwise, be lent, re-sold, hired or otherwise circulated without the publisher's prior consent in any form of binding or cover other than that in which it is published and without a similar condition including this condition being imposed on the subsequent purchaser. The book is published at a net price, and is supplied subject to the Publishers Association Standard Conditions of Sale registered under the Restrictive Trade Practices Act, 1956.

Angela Davies

Panorama of History Series

The Industrial Revolution

Keith Dawson

 Pan Books Ltd : London

Published 1972 by Pan Books Ltd,
33 Tothill Street, London, SW1.

ISBN 0 330 02993 2

(c) Marshall Cavendish U.S.A. Limited, 1972

The material contained in this book is based on
material first published in 'History Makers'.

This book may not be sold in the United States
of America or Canada.

Printed by Proost, Turnhout, Belgium.

Picture Credits

A. F. Kersting   22
Bristol City Art Gallery   B 10
By kind permission of the Earl of Leicester   T 10
Chris Barker   8/9, 11, 18, 20, 21, 28, 31, 35, 44, 49, 52, 56
Chris Barker; by kind permission of the Kirk Museum York   12, 13
Chris Barker / Museum, Halifax   27
Chris Barker / Science Museum, London Front Cover, 33, L34
Cunard Line   62
Cy Fartha Castle Museum, Merthyr Tydfil, South Wales   39
Diagram   14/15, 16, 17, 23, 24, 25, 38, 40, 41, 42
Illustrated London News   50
Mansell   48, 60
Mary Evans Picture Library   19, R34, 45, 46, 57
National Museum of Wales / painting by G. Robertson   30
Parker Gallery, London   7
Picturepoint   37
Queen Park Gallery, Manchester / painting by Eyre Crowe   54
Radio Times Hulton Picture Library   63
Trades Union Congress   58/59, 61
Weinreb & Douwma Ltd., London   26, 29, (cartoon by James Gillray)   55

Contents

The Britain that vanished

During the Industrial revolution, the vision, daring, and inventiveness of individual human beings made Britain the 'Workshop of the World' — but at a social cost with which she never quite came to terms. Craftsmen, engineers and businessmen launched the great social, scientific, and economic revolution that within eighty years transformed Britain almost beyond recognition.

Above: *Engraving of Bloomsbury Square, showing the pleasant country atmosphere of a town before open spaces were replaced by red brick.* **Below:** *Agricultural labourers threshing corn. Before the Revolution most of the British labour force worked in agriculture.*

Industrial society is so familiar to us that it requires a great imaginative effort to realize that until about 150 years ago it simply had not begun to exist. The grandparents of old people living today were born (around 1820) at the dividing time between what we think of as normal life and what all people before them knew was normal. Industrial society was launched in this country in the short space of about seventy years between 1760 and 1830. These are not exact dates but they may serve as a rough guide to pinpoint the Industrial Revolution. A single life span witnessed the most remarkable change in the history of mankind.

What was England like for a child born in the middle of the 18th century? There can be no one answer. It would depend very much on where he was born and into which class of society. Each county had its own characteristics, each town its own civic pride and its own history. It is best perhaps to think of pre-industrial England as almost a federation of counties with very marked local differences. Eighty per cent of the population lived on the land, whose cultivation rarely gave them much rest. They relied on primitive farming methods to keep themselves and the rest of society from food shortage or even starvation. This was the life of which George Crabbe wrote:

'Lo! where the heath, with withering brake grown o'er,
Lends the light turf that warms the neighbouring poor;
From thence a length of burning sand appears,
Where the thin harvest waves its withered ears;
Rank weeds, that every art and care defy,
Reign o'er the land, and rob the blighted rye:

7

There thistles stretch their prickly arms afar,
And to the ragged infant threaten war;
There poppies nodding, mock the hope of toil;
There the blue bugloss paints the sterile soil;

'Here joyless roam a wild amphibious race,
With sullen woe displayed in every face;
Who far from civil arts and social fly,
And scowl at strangers with suspicious eye.'

There is evidence to support Crabbe's view. Arthur Young, that much-travelled commentator on rural life, wrote in 1773:

'I am clear there are at least 600,000 waste acres in the single county of Northumberland. In those of Cumberland and Westmoreland, there are as many more. In the North and part of the West Riding of Yorkshire, and the contiguous ones of Lancashire and in the west part of Durham are yet greater tracts; you may draw a line from the north point of Derbyshire, to the extremity of Northumberland, of 150 miles as the crow flies, which shall be entirely across waste lands; the exception of small cultivated spots very trifling. The East Riding of Yorkshire, Lincolnshire, Cambridgeshire, Dorsetshire, have large tracts; Devonshire, Cornwall, and all Wales immense ones. The greater part of Scotland, unimproved. To these may be added a long catalogue of forests, heaths, downs, chases, and other wastes scattered through the other Counties, and even within sight of the capital; forming altogether a monstrous proportion, even of the whole territory.'

Despite this awful wastage of potential resources, England was an extremely rich agricultural country. From the Middle Ages sheep-farming had flourished to meet the needs of the principal export – wool and woollen cloth. After the Dissolution of the Monasteries in the 16th century, large areas of new land came on to the market. Large landowners put their sheep on them, and as a result there was a boom in the wool trade. Gradually spare land was used up so that in the Midlands the traditional open fields were taken over by enterprising farmers who enclosed the land for grazing. This process was carried

Giant symbol of industrialization – one of the first colliery winding-machines in England.

Above: *Thomas Coke — a pioneer in new methods of sheep-farming and cultivation. Before the Revolution the wool trade was Britain's major industry.* **Below:** *Painting of Brood Quay, Bristol, in the early 18th century. The large and prosperous seaport of Bristol second city in the land, had grown rich on the trade in slaves.*

further in the 18th century when as a result of thousands of private Acts of Parliament a broad band of the country from Yorkshire, Lincolnshire, and Norfolk, through the Midland counties to the south coast was affected by enclosure.

It was a piecemeal process, relying entirely on private initiative, and it came in response to the growing needs of the towns and from a desire to profit from more efficient methods of cultivation and breeding which were being adopted by men like Coke of Norfolk, who transformed the sandy wastes of his estates at Holkham into rich wheatlands; Lord Townshend, the most celebrated of those who experimented with improving rotation of crops, including the famous turnip so useful in stock-rearing; Robert Bakewell, whose systematic breeding of sheep for mutton in Leicestershire had remarkable results and whose methods were used by the Colling brothers on cattle to make the Durham shorthorns famous. Improvements were far from widespread but they were enough to make England an outstanding farming country, much visited by foreigners in search of ideas.

Such improvements accelerated the development of local specialization throughout the country. (Few Englishmen relied solely on subsistence farming; most produced something for local market sale.) No town exerted a greater influence than London. The 'whole kingdom,' wrote Defoe, 'as well the people, as the land, and even the sea, in every part of it, are employ'd to furnish something, and I may add, the best of everything, to supply the city of London with provisions'. So, even before the 18th century, London was receiving geese and capons from Sussex and Surrey and turkeys from Suffolk, fruit from Kent and Worcestershire, cheeses and other dairy produce from Cheshire, Wiltshire, and Suffolk, and cattle from Leicestershire. Bristol, the second city in the land, exerted a similar influence on the land about it, receiving butter from Pembroke, eggs and milk from Wiltshire, cheese from Cheshire, and peas and beans from Gloucestershire.

Town and country in pre-industrial Britain

It is tempting to look for the origins of industrial society in the towns, as towns have grown with industry. With a few notable exceptions it would be a mistake to do so. Most towns in the 18th century were little more than a market for the surrounding countryside and the local rich. They provided a market, a few shops, one or two inns for travellers and probably an Assembly

The Merchant Adventurers, one of the two oldest English chartered companies, was founded in the early 15th century and was chiefly engaged in the export of wool. It brought riches to many northern towns. York, prior to 1800 was one of the wealthiest cities in the land and the Merchant Adventurers' Hall, built in 1387, is still the company's home, although its heyday was over long before the Industrial Revolution.

Room where local functions would be held and bands of travelling players would perform from time to time. As the population of even quite flourishing smaller towns was between 2,000 and 4,000, it will be obvious that they were hardly distinct from the surrounding countryside. Writing of the 1820s Thomas Hardy in *The Mayor of Casterbridge* captures the atmosphere of an English country town before the Industrial Revolution:

'It was compact as a box of dominoes. It had no suburbs – in the ordinary sense. Country and town met at a mathematical line . . .

'The agricultural and pastoral character of the people upon whom the town depended for its existence was shown by the class of objects displayed in the shop windows. Scythes, reap-hooks, sheep-shears, bill-hooks, spades, mattocks, and hoes at the ironmongers; bee-hives, butter-firkins, churns, milking stools and pails, hay-rakes, field flagons, and seed-lips at the cooper's; cart-ropes and plough harness at the saddler's; carts, wheel-barrows, and mill-gear at the wheelwright's and machinist's; horse-embrocations at the chemist's; at the glover's and leather-cutter's, hedging-gloves, thatchers' knee-caps, ploughmen's leggings, villagers' pattens and clogs . . .

'Casterbridge was the complement of the rural life around; not its urban opposite. Bees and butterflies in the cornfields at the top of the town, who desired to get to the meads at the bottom, took no circuitous course, but flew straight down the High Street without any apparent consciousness that they were traversing strange latitudes.'

As the towns grew larger, they provided a market where not only important gentlemen landowners but also enterprising small farmers could make a very good living. Rural society, however, had not been much affected by this growing market, and the social structure in 1760 was much as it had been for at least 200 years. This was the framework within which the vast majority of the people of England lived, as revealed by Gregory King who produced his conclusions in 1688, 113 years before the first official census. (See diagrams on pages 14-15). Though the social groups which King indentifies were not water-tight (it was far easier to move up or down society in England than for example in France), they do represent categories which would have been universally recognized at the time. Despite the money that some people were undoubtedly making out of the land, most people had to be content with the position on the social scale into which they had been born – 'The rich man in his castle, the poor man at his gate', although that hymn is a Victorian survival of the same idea.

At the top was the ruling élite of nobility and gentry, for whose comfort and entertainment society really existed. Their estates, their country-houses, great and small, with their surrounding gardens and parkland were oases of opulence and sometimes culture in what was for the majority a desert of poverty. The gentry ran the country, largely though not entirely in their own interests, either from Parliament at Westminster or more directly from their estates where they controlled the district as Justices of the Peace and as general benefactors. Below them the freeholders ploughed an independent and often profitable furrow, and the mass of labourers toiled to earn as a class rather less than they needed to support life. Such, apparently, was the will of God, the natural order of society which had existed beyond memory. Its end was imminent in the middle of the 18th century, but this would have been scarcely credible to our ancestors.

Only two of the great towns of pre-industrial England have survived as important urban centres today – London and Bristol. London is unique and always has been. Two hundred years ago, with a population of about 800,000, it housed one in ten of the people of Great Britain and dominated the economic life of the nation just as it does today. Bristol, well placed for the Atlantic, had grown rich on the trade in slaves and other more reputable merchandise. The other major centres of the Industrial Revolution – Birmingham, Manchester, Leeds, Liverpool, etc. developed as towns only during the 18th century, and, purpose - built for industry, surged ahead of famous old towns like York and Norwich (as seen from the population maps and diagrams on pages 14-16). They presented an unprepared 19th century with the awful problems of making an industrial environment tolerable.

Evolution or Revolution

It is not enough simply to observe the growth of new towns and the changing character of industry if we are to explain why the revolution occurred when it did. Such an enormous event must involve the economy as a whole and have its roots deep in the past. Before the Industrial Revolution England's wealth came mainly from the land and from trade, but industry did exist to such a degree that some historians have argued that the whole idea of a revolution in the late 18th century is an illusion.

Tools and workshop of a comb-maker. Before the coming of factories, craftsmen worked at home at their own pace, and often owned their own tools. Machines spelt ruin for many such local cottage industries.

Candle-making, once a purely domestic art, was a specialized craft by medieval times, with two livery companies in London. Joseph Morgan invented the prototype of the modern candle-moulding machine in 1834 — another example of an ancient craft eroded by industralization.

This industry was not simply the familiar craft sort where a master craftsman presided over a family consisting of his wife and children, one or two journeymen, and an apprentice or two and all combined together to perform the 'mysteries' of their trade. The traditional organization of industry, ideal for small-scale operations in a fairly static society, was already breaking down by the 18th century. Where new towns developed, the guilds found it virtually impossible to extend their control and bigger industries, like cloth, or new industries, like mining and metallurgy, could hardly be organized in this way. Great developments took place in these latter industries in the century following the Reformation, the period of the first great inflation in England from about 1540 to 1640 when for the first time enterprising men could make fortunes quickly.

The tremendous expansion in the cloth industry in the 16th century led to reorganization on capitalist lines. True, there were virtually no technical innovations, apart from the stocking-frame, and no factories in the conventional sense existed, but the 'putting-out' system, where spinners and weavers would work raw wool or yarn in their homes, became a very large-scale organization. A big clothier might employ 1,000 workers which required considerable capital and quite complicated systems of distribution and collection. Capitalism was even more obvious in other industries. It might cost around £1,000 (worth roughly thirty times the equivalent sum today), simply to sink a shaft, but once shafts were sunk, mining became a capitalist enterprise. Collieries existed in the late 16th century which were producing 10,000 to 25,000 tons a year and these required the investment of many thousands of pounds. A glance at Gregory King's estimate of income will make it obvious that this was a heavy outlay even for the richest members of the community at the end of the 17th century.

Considerable investment was necessary in many other industries which developed in the period. A London brewery in the early 17th century had a capital of £10,000. Thousands of pounds were necessary to equip new ironworks with very solid blast-furnaces thirty feet high, gigantic leathern bellows, and ducted water to supply power. A smelting-works at Keswick employed 4,000 men around 1640. Brick-making, sugar-refining, soap-boiling, salt-works, and other similar processes all came to use coal and cost their owners considerable sums for the necessary pans, vats, pipes, and furnaces.

1. Estimate of population and wealth in 1688

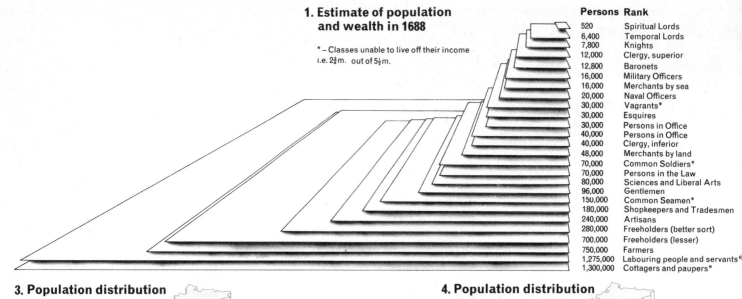

* – Classes unable to live off their income i.e. 2¾m. out of 5½m.

Persons	Rank
520	Spiritual Lords
6,400	Temporal Lords
7,800	Knights
12,000	Clergy, superior
12,800	Baronets
16,000	Military Officers
16,000	Merchants by sea
20,000	Naval Officers
30,000	Vagrants*
30,000	Esquires
30,000	Persons in Office
40,000	Persons in Office
40,000	Clergy, inferior
48,000	Merchants by land
70,000	Common Soldiers*
70,000	Persons in the Law
80,000	Sciences and Liberal Arts
96,000	Gentlemen
150,000	Common Seamen*
180,000	Shopkeepers and Tradesmen
240,000	Artisans
280,000	Freeholders (better sort)
700,000	Freeholders (lesser)
750,000	Farmers
1,275,000	Labouring people and servants
1,300,000	Cottagers and paupers*

3. Population distribution 1701

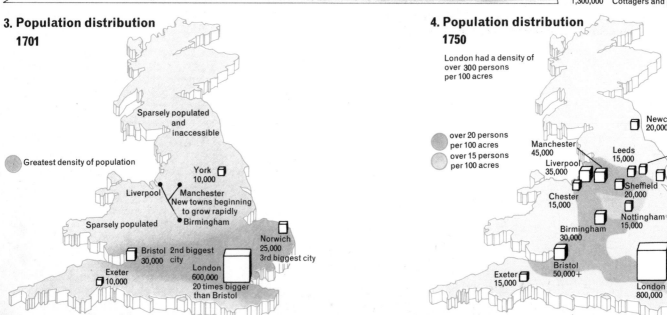

Sparsely populated and inaccessible

Greatest density of population

York 10,000

Liverpool

Manchester

New towns beginning to grow rapidly

Birmingham

Sparsely populated

Bristol 30,000 2nd biggest city

Norwich 25,000 3rd biggest city

Exeter 10,000

London 600,000 20 times bigger than Bristol

4. Population distribution 1750

London had a density of over 300 persons per 100 acres

over 20 persons per 100 acres

over 15 persons per 100 acres

Newcastle 20,000

Manchester 45,000

Leeds 15,000

York 15,000

Liverpool 35,000

Hull 20,000

Sheffield 20,000

Chester 15,000

Nottingham 15,000

Birmingham 30,000

Norwich 35,000

Bristol 50,000+

Exeter 15,000

London 800,000

early Income per Family Figures in pounds

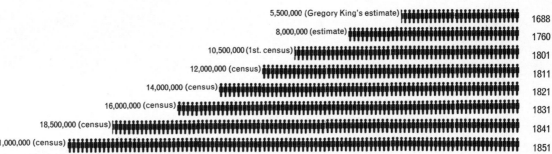

,300	
,800	
50	
0	
80	
0	
00	
50	
20	
40	
5	
00	
4	
40	
0	
80	
0	
5	
0	
4	
0	
4	
5	
½	

2. Population growth

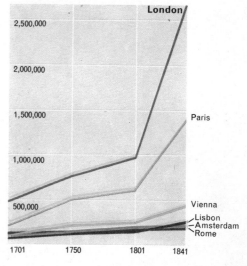

5,500,000 (Gregory King's estimate)	1688
8,000,000 (estimate)	1760
10,500,000 (1st. census)	1801
12,000,000 (census)	1811
14,000,000 (census)	1821
16,000,000 (census)	1831
18,500,000 (census)	1841
21,000,000 (census)	1851

5. Population distribution

1801

London had a density of
over 400 persons
per 100 acres

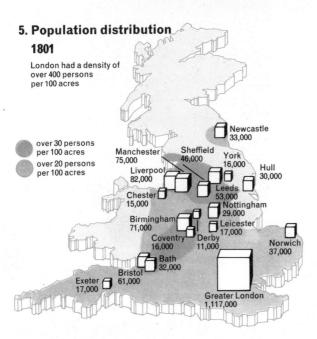

over 30 persons
per 100 acres

over 20 persons
per 100 acres

Newcastle
33,000

Manchester
75,000

Sheffield
46,000

York
16,000

Hull
30,000

Liverpool
82,000

Chester
15,000

Leeds
53,000

Nottingham
29.000

Birmingham
71,000

Leicester
17,000

Coventry
16,000

Derby
11,000

Norwich
37,000

Bath
32,000

Bristol
61,000

Exeter
17,000

Greater London
1,117,000

6. London and European Cities 1700-1840

London

2,500,000

2,000,000

1,500,000

Paris

1,000,000

Vienna

500,000

Lisbon
Amsterdam
Rome

1701   1750   1801   1841

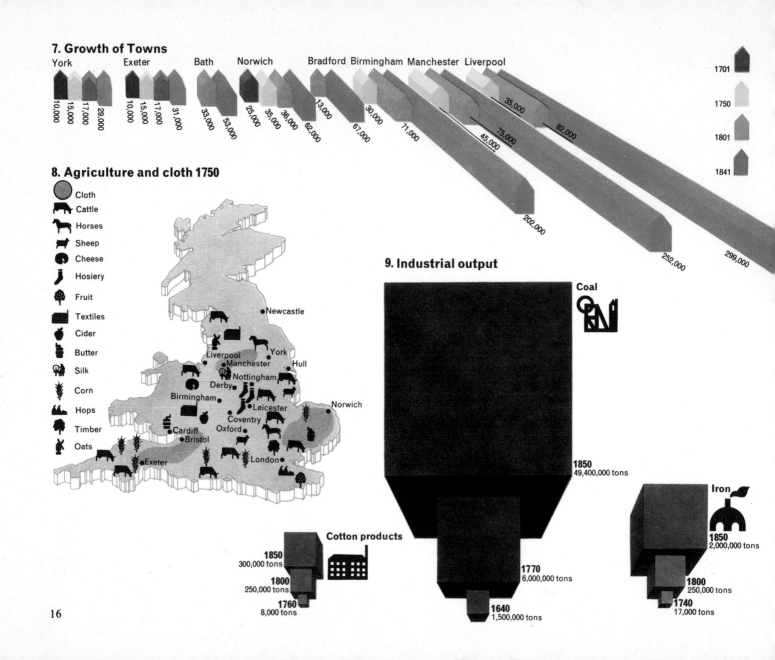

7. Growth of Towns

York — 10,000 · 15,000 · 17,000 · 29,000
Exeter — 10,000 · 15,000 · 17,000 · 31,000
Bath — 33,000 · 53,000
Norwich — 25,000 · 35,000 · 36,000 · 62,000
Bradford — 13,000 · 67,000
Birmingham — 30,000 · 71,000
Manchester — 75,000 · 45,000 · 202,000
Liverpool — 35,000 · 82,000 · 252,000 · 299,000

1701
1750
1801
1841

8. Agriculture and cloth 1750

- Cloth
- Cattle
- Horses
- Sheep
- Cheese
- Hosiery
- Fruit
- Textiles
- Cider
- Butter
- Silk
- Corn
- Hops
- Timber
- Oats

Newcastle
Liverpool
York
Manchester
Hull
Nottingham
Derby
Birmingham
Leicester
Norwich
Coventry
Cardiff
Oxford
Bristol
Exeter
London

9. Industrial output

Coal

1850 49,400,000 tons
1770 6,000,000 tons
1640 1,500,000 tons

Cotton products

1850 300,000 tons
1800 250,000 tons
1760 8,000 tons

Iron

1850 2,000,000 tons
1800 250,000 tons
1740 17,000 tons

16

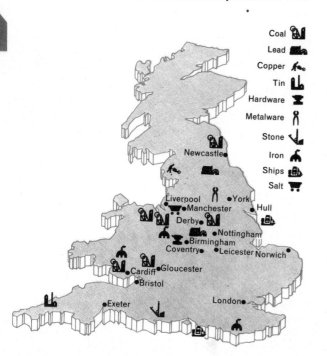

10. Main industrial products 1750

Coal
Lead
Copper
Tin
Hardware
Metalware
Stone
Iron
Ships
Salt

Newcastle

Liverpool • York
Manchester • Hull
Derby •
Nottingham
Birmingham
Coventry • Leicester Norwich •
Cardiff • Gloucester
Bristol
Exeter
London •

Such impressive changes have been called the 'industrial revolution' of the 16th century, but it is a mistake to do so. John Cleveland might cry 'Correct your maps: Newcastle is Peru!' early in the 17th century, but coal's equivalent of the solid silver Peruvian mountain Potosi was not properly tapped until well into the 19th. Set beside 19th century output, the achievements of the 17th century look very small indeed. Coal output, at 1,500,000 tons in 1640, was double that of the rest of Europe but, even though production increased steadily to reach 6,000,000 tons in 1770, this increase was small compared with the 23,000,000 tons reached in 1830 and the almost 50,000,000 tons of twenty years later. Iron production actually went down in the late 17th century. Furnaces burnt charcoal at this time and the forests of England were rapidly used up. By 1739 only sixty furnaces were working in the whole country to produce a mere 17,000 tons of iron a year. If there really had been an industrial revolution in the 17th century, such a collapse of iron production would have been impossible. There was a revival in the next forty years but the usefulness of the 68,000 tons produced by 1788 cannot be compared with the 250,000 tons produced in 1800 or the 1,000,000 tons in 1835.

The rate of growth and the enormous scale of production are the essential features of the Industrial Revolution. It was like the second stage of a rocket which shot the economy clear of the gravitational pull which had prevented production from rising freely in the earlier stage. It enabled the economy to achieve what has been called 'self-sustained growth'.

Until recently, industry has needed masses of workers and there is no doubt that the remarkable increase in the population from the last third of the 18th century onwards provided the necessary labour. But population alone cannot explain the revolution. China and India have both had population explosions but the result has been widespread poverty rather than the coming of industry. Moreover, if a greater proportion of the population were to be working full-time in industry, the land would have to yield far more food, far more efficiently. It was lucky that the improvements in agriculture mentioned earlier came in time. Besides manpower, industry needs an abundance of capital to set it up and easily available credit for long-term investment. Here, too, England was fortunate for the growth of her world-wide commercial empire and the expansion of the European market had made her the richest trading empire in the

Bricks were formerly moulded by hand after piles of clay had been weathered out of doors. Mechanization was well advanced by 1850 and mills such as this were soon playing their part in transforming the face of England's 'green and pleasant land'.

world. Quite sophisticated banking organizations had developed from the end of the 17th century to help the growth of trade and these could equally well help industry.

No one would think of investing large sums of money in industry, however, unless they could be sure of opening up useful markets. A modest but clear rise in incomes, especially among the real consumers of the time – the middle and upper classes – both in Britain and Europe made for a demand which in some industries ran ahead of supply and acted as a spur to invention. America, too, was a good growing market. Even the War of Independence could not stop the growth of trade between the two countries. Each relied on the other, America for British consumer goods, Britain for American raw materials, notably and increasingly cotton.

But perhaps the most basic need was decent transport, and this will be the starting-point for the next chapter. The roads of England around 1700 were incredibly bad and the rivers did not provide a connected system of transport. As a result most of the heavy traffic had to be sent by sea round the coast and though this helped places like Hull and Newcastle to flourish, it was of little use to inland areas. It was fortunate for the future of British industry that turnpike roads, river improvement, and canal-building were well under way by the latter part of the 18th century.

With all these impersonal forces at work, it is refreshing to be able to say that above all the Industrial Revolution rested on the vision, the daring, and the inventiveness of individual human beings. It did not emerge, as a result of a vast bureaucratic plan, backed by immense Government spending. The Government, largely composed as it was of people with a vested interest in the land, remained almost wholly indifferent to the growth of industry. That great work was left to practical businessmen, inventors and engineers of great skill and sometimes genius who often joined forces with visionary aristocrats who could foresee a Britain very different from the rural peace and poverty and ignorance amid which they lived. Such a one was the Duke of Bridgewater who gave James Brindley, the semi-literate son of a Derbyshire crofter his head so that he produced masterpieces of canal-building which were marvels not only for their time but also by any modern standards.

The Take-off

The Industrial Revolution began with the cloth industry. The cloth-mills and the clatter of new looms were its heralds. But behind this industrial take-off was another revolution — the transport revolution. For the first time in history it became possible to move goods with reasonable speed from one part of the country to another.

Victorian engraving of travellers waiting to pay at a turnpike. The commissioners were after accused of neglecting to repair the roads — they 'put the toll of the poor cheated passenger in their pockets, and, leave every jolt as bad as they find it, if not worse'.

'Suppose you take the . . . northern road, namely, by St. Albans, Dunstable, Hockley, Newport Pagnel, Northampton, Leicester, and Nottingham, or Darby: On this road, after you are pass'd Dunstable, which is about thirty miles, you enter the deep clays, which are so surprisingly soft, that it is perfectly frightful to travellers, and it has been the wonder of foreigners, how, considering the great numbers of carriages which are continually passing with heavy loads, those ways have been made practicable; indeed the great number of horses every year kill'd by the excess of labour in those heavy ways, has been such a charge on the country, that new building of causeways, as the Romans did of old, seems to me to be a much easier expence.'

So wrote Daniel Defoe in his *A Tour thro' the Whole Island of Great Britain*, first published in 1726. This book, and others of the period, paint a frightful picture of the state of English roads. Defoe tells us that another major highway 'is not passable but just in the middle of summer, after the coal carriages have beaten the way, for the ground is a stiff clay, so after rain the water stands as in a dish, and the horses sink in up to their bellies'. Other roads were almost blocked by huge rocks, often put there to repair the surface. Roads were often so narrow that the banks and hedges towered above them and so worn that 'the stag, the hounds and the huntsmen have been known to leap over a loaded waggon in a hollow way without any obstruction from the vehicle'. Such were the results of 1,400 years of neglect. The Romans had built a network of fine roads during their occupation of the British Isles. They were fine engineers and they built well, but without systematic maintenance or periodic reconstruction even their roads could not hope to survive. The

Thomas Telford (1757-1834) was responsible for building a network of roads through the Scottish Highlands as well as many canals and bridges throughout Britain, including the two suspension bridges over the River Conway and the Menai Straits. The Pontcysyllte Aqueduct in Denbighshire is also his work. With its nineteen arches, it carries the Ellesmere Canal 120 feet high over the River Dee.

result was that road travel in the 18th century was slow, dirty, and dangerous. The few stage-coaches that made the journey in 1700 took a week to travel from London to York, and those brave enough to make the trip would certainly have an extremely uncomfortable time, even if they were lucky enough not to have the coach overturn in a rut or to avoid being robbed by one of the ruffian highwaymen, so different in reality from the romantic figures of legend.

No country with a road system like this could possibly hope for the great industrial advance that England enjoyed at the end of the 18th century. Good communications of all sorts are necessary for goods to be transported quickly, reliably, and cheaply and in this respect England was well behind France around 1700. Bad though they were, however, the roads of England had to cope with a fairly heavy traffic in all manner of industrial and agricultural produce. Droves of cattle, sheep, and pigs were driven long distances to the market at Smithfield; geese and turkeys in their thousands were brought to market from perhaps 100 miles away, feeding as they came on the crops in the roadside fields. Where roads were particularly bad, merchants sent their goods on pack-horses. Wool and yarn were distributed by pack-horse in south Lancashire and the West Riding of Yorkshire, and even coal was carried in this way by mountain paths from Merthyr to Cardiff. Some attempts were made to use heavy wagons, but the following passage from Defoe shows clearly the impossible situation caused by the state of the roads. 'The timber I saw here [around Lewes] was prodigious, as well in quantity as in bigness, and seem'd in some places to be suffer'd to grow, only because it was not worth cutting down and carrying away; in dry summers, indeed, a great deal is carry'd away to Maidstone, and other places on the Medway; and sometimes I have seen one tree on a carriage, which they here call a tug, drawn by two and twenty oxen, and even then, 'tis carry'd so little a way, and then thrown down, and left for other tugs to take up and carry on, that sometimes 'tis two or three year before it gets to Chatham; for if once the rains come in, it stirs not more that year, and sometimes the whole summer is not dry enough to make the roads passable.'

Clearly, the roads were not fit even to cope with the traffic of pre-industrial England. It was fortunate for the future prosperity of the country that great improvements were made in the middle of the century by the setting up of Turnpike Trusts. This was a

Above: *The Bridgewater warehouse on the Manchester-Worsley Canal, the first canal built by the extraordinary partnership of the Duke of Bridgewater and James Brindley. It cut transport costs by half, and was the beginning of a revolution in communications.*
Below: *John Metcalf began his road-building career with this bridge at Boroughbridge.*

system of private enterprise whereby a board of trustees was granted, in a private Act of Parliament, the right to construct and maintain a particular piece of road. The trustees raised loans to pay for the work of construction and repaid the interest on the loan by charging tolls to those who used their road. A trust would usually run for twenty-one years, during which time the board would be free to operate as it wished. The first turnpikes came into existence at the end of the 17th century, but they only became common after the Young Pretender's Rebellion in 1745 had shown the government how inadequate the roads were for troop movements. Between 1750 and 1790 some 1,600 Acts of Parliament were passed to extend and improve the turnpike system which came to control over 18,000 miles of roads in England and 24,500 in the United Kingdom.

Naturally the trusts were not all conscientious or efficient and there were widespread criticisms by travellers and officials of the Board of Agriculture, set up in 1793. Lord Hervey wrote to Lady Mary Wortley Montagu in 1743, '... the commissioners for most other turnpikes seldom execute what they undertake; they only put the toll of the poor cheated passenger in their pockets, and leave every jolt as bad as they find it, if not worse'. Twenty-five years later Arthur Young wrote that the road from Witney to Northleach 'is, I think, the worst turnpike I ever travelled in; so bad that it is a scandal to the country. They mend and make with nothing but the stone which forms the under stratum all over the country ... by using it alone, and in pieces as large as one's head, the road is rendered most execrable.'

Such criticisms continued through to the 19th century but they hide the very real improvements that were being made throughout the period. Defoe prophesied that ''tis more than probable, that our posterity may see the roads all over England restor'd in their time, to such a perfection, that travelling and carriage of goods will be much more easy both to man and horse, than ever it was since the Romans lost this island', and much of this had been accomplished by the early 19th century. The journey from Leeds to London took only twenty-one hours in 1815 compared with the seven days' crawl from London to York in 1700; the time taken from London to Manchester was reduced from four and a half days to twenty-eight hours between 1754 and 1788. Such speeds encouraged travel. New coach routes developed regular services; mail-coaches became much more frequent and reliable, and exercised a powerful influence on road

Thomas Telford was surely the leading European engineer of his time. His graceful suspension bridge over the Conway in North Wales sets off the solid thirteenth-century castle.

construction; wagons replaced pack-horses in the carriage of goods, and a wagon service would transport a tradesman's goods from Lancashire or Yorkshire to London in a matter of thirty-six hours. This was a great stimulus to trade.

The best roads at this time were largely built by three men who laid the basis for roads which could cope with the demands of an industrial society – John Metcalf (1717–1810), John Loudon McAdam (1756–1836), and Thomas Telford (1757–1834). Metcalf ('Blind Jack of Knaresborough' as he was called) was an amazing man. Born of poor parents, he lost his sight at the age of six after a smallpox attack. Yet he was an accomplished violinist and a fine athlete and jockey. He quickly became a well-known figure in the small town of Knaresborough and at the age of twenty-two he eloped with a publican's daughter, Dorothy Benson, on the eve of her wedding to another man, only to return to Knaresborough with his bride and settle down as a good husband and respected horse-dealer. While still in his twenties he walked to London and back, easily beating a coach on the return journey. Before turning his attention to roads in 1765, when he was forty-eight years old, he had turned his hand successfully to cotton and worsted trading, smuggling, and stage-coaching – running a service between York and Knaresborough.

The great road builders

Metcalf began his road-building career by improving three miles of road on the new Harrogate to Boroughbridge Turnpike and building a bridge at Boroughbridge. Thereafter, he constructed 180 miles of turnpike in Yorkshire and Lancashire including roads linking Wakefield and Doncaster, Huddersfield and Halifax, Bury and Blackburn, Ashton and Stockport and, most astonishingly, Huddersfield and Manchester – the last being over a bog previously thought to be impassable. It seems incredible that a totally blind man should be capable of such feats, but he had an uncanny sense of terrain, an amazing memory, and boundless energy. Armed only with a long staff, he marched over the hills and valleys of the backbone of England, exploring possibilities and calculating in his head by a method of his own which he was incapable of explaining properly to others. Before he died at the age of ninety-three, leaving behind him over ninety great-grandchildren, he had laid the foundations of a fine road system in the new home of the textile industry.

The revolution of speed

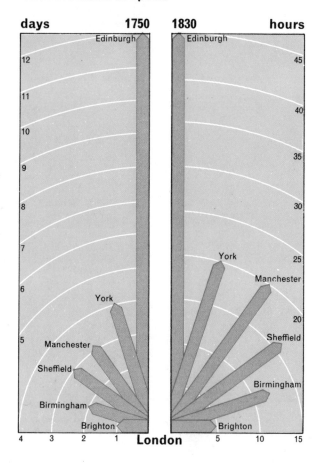

days | 1750 | 1830 | hours

London

McAdam's contribution to the new roads was a new surface. Of independent means, he bought an estate at Sauhrie in Ayrshire, where he was able to experiment with various surfaces. He said that existing roads were 'loose, rough and perishable, expensive, tedious, and dangerous to travel on, and very costly to repair', and the solution he produced reversed most current practices. 'The first operation in making a road,' he said, 'should be the reverse of digging a trench. The roads should not be sunk below, but rather raised above the ordinary level of the adjacent ground; care should at any rate be taken that there be a sufficient fall to take off the water, so that it should always be some inches below the level of the ground upon which the road is intended to be placed. . . .' The raised roadway should be built up by thin layers of hard dry stone, broken to a maximum weight of six ounces, which would then be packed down into a hard, impervious surface, free of soil and clay, by the passing traffic. This simple solution revolutionized roads, not only in England, but throughout the world. It helped materially to develop fast and reliable stage- and mail-coach services, and McAdam was able to supervise developments, first locally after 1815 when he was Surveyor-General of Bristol roads, and later nationally as General Surveyor of Roads after 1827. Before his death, his name (mis-spelt) was universally used for the new surface.

McAdam's surface was a development of those used by Telford, but there is no doubt that it was Telford who made the greatest contribution to the improvements in transport. Like Metcalf, he came from a very poor home. His father, a Dumfriesshire shepherd, died when Telford was still a baby, so that the boy had to work herding cattle when still very young. But he was always active and lively and he managed to pick up a basic education in the three Rs. As he grew older he developed a taste for poetry and his own work was praised by Robert Southey. Trained as a mason, he came to have an interest in all forms of transport and his first work on roads was done in Scotland, which he was commissioned to survey in 1801. The result of fifteen years' work was over 900 miles of good road in Scotland which involved the construction of 120 bridges to span the many fast-flowing rivers. Telford's bridges are works of art, blending superbly with the surrounding countryside, as well as masterly pieces of engineering. His other important road improvements were the Glasgow to Carlisle road built between 1814 and 1825, and the London to Holyhead road (1810–30) built for the Post Office and requiring the construction

23

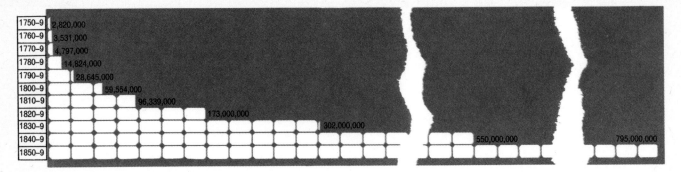

Imports of cotton wool Annual average per decade. Amount in lb.

1750–9	2,820,000
1760–9	3,531,000
1770–9	4,797,000
1780–9	14,824,000
1790–9	28,645,000
1800–9	59,554,000
1810–9	96,339,000
1820–9	173,000,000
1830–9	302,000,000
1840–9	550,000,000
1850–9	795,000,000

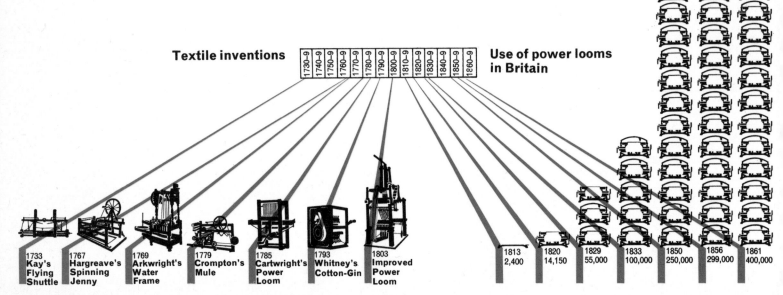

Textile inventions

1730–9 1740–9 1750–9 1760–9 1770–9 1780–9 1790–9 1800–9 1810–9 1820–9 1830–9 1840–9 1850–9 1860–9

Use of power looms in Britain

1733 Kay's Flying Shuttle
1767 Hargreave's Spinning Jenny
1769 Arkwright's Water Frame
1779 Crompton's Mule
1785 Cartwright's Power Loom
1793 Whitney's Cotton-Gin
1803 Improved Power Loom

1813 2,400
1820 14,150
1829 55,000
1833 100,000
1850 250,000
1856 299,000
1861 400,000

Canals and waterways

Firth of Forth

River Tyne

Firth of Clyde
Solway Firth

River Mersey
River Dee

Bridgewater
Canal

Grand
Trunk
Canal

Ellesmere
Canal

River Humber

Birmingham
Canal

Grand
Junction
Canal

River
Thames

River Severn
Bristol Channel

of the famous Menai Bridge.

Canals and rivers

Important though the road improvements were in speeding transport and allowing far more goods to travel longer distances, the crucial change in transport before the railway revolution was the dramatic opening up of a national system of water transport. Britain has many rivers which are easy to navigate, and the map shows how the important estuaries on the east and west coasts are almost linked by rivers – the Firth of Clyde and the Firth of Forth; the Solway Firth and the Tyne; the Mersey and the Humber; the Bristol Channel and the Thames. Yet before 1700 very little had been done to link these together. The Stour and the Avon had been deepened and the Mersey had been made navigable as far as Warrington but little else had been done. This was at a time when the Dutch had very fine waterways and the French had constructed three important canals – between the Seine and the Loire (1640); the Canal of the Two Seas linking Toulouse and Cette (1681); and the Orleans Canal (1692). It may be that, with fine ports, inland waterways in England had not seemed 'necessary, but by the middle of the century increasing production, particularly of coal, led landowners who possessed coal-fields to press for river improvements and canals. As a result rivers near Wigan and St Helens were improved and schemes were made for canals between Salford and Wigan and St Helens and Liverpool. Water transport might be slow but it was the only practical way of carrying huge loads before the coming of the railways.

The breakthrough in water transport came as a result of the combined efforts of an English aristocrat and an almost illiterate genius from Derbyshire: the Duke of Bridgewater and James Brindley. Like so many of the pioneers of the Industrial Revolution, Brindley had to fight his way through an unpromising boyhood. He was shielded from an idle father by a careful mother, but he was himself accused of idleness by the millwright at Macclesfield to whom he was apprenticed, and he was nearly returned to his home as a failure. He soon proved his engineering ability, however, by installing complicated machinery into a paper-mill, and he moved to Leek in Staffordshire where he spent fifteen years in the repairing business and experimenting with steam-engines, until he was called by Bridgewater in 1759 to help plan a canal from his Worsley coal-mines to Manchester.

Cartwright, Radcliffe and Horrocks were the men who sealed the fate of hand-loom weavers such as this one, shown spinning and and winding wool, in an 18th century picture. By 1813 there were some 100 power looms operating throughout the country.

Bridgewater, too, had had a poor start. His family had thought him feeble-minded and had considered depriving him of his inheritance, and it was only after he had failed to make his mark in London that he returned to Old Hall, Worsley, at the end of 1758. From then, he devoted his entire life to making his estates a great industrial concern. Coal and canals were his only interests. He never married, enjoyed simple, manly pleasures and disliked beauty and ornament even to the extent of lopping off the heads of flowers which had been planted on one occasion during his absence in London.

The coal-mines at Worsley made Bridgewater one of the largest coal-owners in the country and yet in 1759 his coal was being transported on horseback at a cost of 9s. to 10s. a ton. It was to reduce these crippling transport costs that Brindley produced imaginative plans for a canal to Manchester which included an aqueduct over the River Irwell. It was completed in 1761 and cut Bridgewater's transport costs by half. The aqueduct became one of the wonders of the nation. A correspondent to the *Annual Register* in 1763 wrote: 'At Barton bridge he has erected a navigable canal in the air; for it is as high as the tops of the trees. Whilst I was surveying it with a mixture of wonder and delight, four barges passed me in the space of about three minutes, two of them being chained together, and dragged by two horses, who went on the terras of the canal, whereon, I must own, I durst hardly venture to walk as I almost trembled to behold the large river Irwell underneath me, across which this navigation is carried by a bridge . . .'

Encouraged by the success of this first venture the Duke of Bridgewater went on to plan a canal from Longford Bridge to Runcorn, linking Manchester and Liverpool which would provide a more effective route than by the Irwell and the Mersey. This was a much more expensive project and it aroused bitter opposition but such was Bridgewater's faith in his engineer that he pledged the now profitable Worsley Canal for £25,000 to meet part of the costs. The first boat, of fifty tons, reached Liverpool by way of this new Bridgewater Canal on the last day of 1772, and before long the cost of transporting goods from Liverpool to Manchester had been reduced from 12s. to 6s. a ton. In all Brindley constructed 365 miles of canals, probably the most important being the Grand Trunk Canal joining the rivers Trent and Mersey which allowed goods from Liverpool to penetrate directly deep into the country and proved an indispensable

Above: *A Scots handloom widely used in the mid 18th century.*
Below: *A semi-mechanized broadloom. These were mostly clumsy, wooden machines which could be used at home. But new, factory-based inventions were soon to take their place.*

lifeline for beer from Burton, salt from Cheshire, and pottery from Staffordshire. It is staggering to note that English canals, the arteries of industrial growth, were started by a man whose wages from his employer were a guinea a week and who was incapable of committing his plans to paper. He did his calculations in his head and when he had a particularly knotty problem he retired to bed to work it out.

Bridgewater lived dangerously in these early years by investing all his estates in his industrial projects. He spent £220,000 on canals alone and he was ultimately rewarded by an annual income from them of £80,000. His vision led other businessmen to invest in canals, and the second half of the 18th century saw the development of a system which knit together the industrial heart of the country by a series of locks, tunnels, and aqueducts. This tremendous achievement – there were nearly 3,000 miles of canals by 1800 – was made in the teeth of resistance from landowners, river boards, and turnpike trustees and without official Government assistance. As J. L. and Barbara Hammond wrote: 'England had solved a problem that had made an industrial revolution impossible in the ancient world, for one of the standing difficulties of that world was the provision of transport for heavy goods otherwise than by sea.'

Next to Brindley, Telford probably made the most important single contribution to canals. In 1763 he was made sole agent, engineer, and architect to construct the Ellesmere Canal which would connect the Mersey, Dee, and Severn. His salary was £500 but out of this he had to pay a clerk and a foreman and also find his own travel expenses. The canal posed great problems, including the need to build aqueducts over the rivers Ceirog and Dee. These vast bridges, 'among the boldest efforts of human invention in modern times', were built by making a bed of cast iron fixed into square stone masonry. The Chirk Aqueduct, over the Ceirog, was opened in 1801 and spanned 700 feet with ten arches 70 feet high, but it was dwarfed by the 1,007-foot Pontcysyllte Aqueduct which carried the canal 120 feet high by means of nineteen superb arches. It was described by Sir Walter Scott as the most impressive work of art he had ever seen. Later, Telford was to build the Caledonian Canal, one of the few to have Government assistance. He also built a new tunnel at Hardcastle Hill on the Grand Junction and made improvements to Brindley's Birmingham Canal.

So as the 18th century flowed into the 19th, goods and

Richard Arkwright, inventor of spinning machinery, built a factory at Cromford, Derbyshire, run by power from a water mill. He went on to build factories in other parts of the country, equipped with machines capable of performing everything from carding to spinning – operations previously done by hand.

correspondence rattled speedily and safely along fine new roads and heavy goods were dragged by horses at about 3 m.p.h. 'so as to provide means for cheap and easy communication from the very heart of each town to every other part of the kingdom and to our chief commercial ports'.

These improvements in communication made possible an explosion in industry. In particular they made it possible for goods to be exported more quickly and efficiently than before. For centuries Britain's chief export had been cloth. But if Britain were to tap the world-wide potential for this material, then, in addition to better communications, moderately expensive innovations and modifications would have to be made to an already thriving industry. New developments in the cloth trade, especially in cotton, would be needed before it became a large-scale factory industry.

Before the Industrial Revolution, cloth was woven almost everywhere in the country, if only for local consumption, but the great areas of production were Yorkshire, centred on Leeds and Halifax; Norfolk, centred on Norwich; and the West Country with a number of important centres. Defoe wrote that Devonshire 'is so full of great towns, and those towns so full of people, and those people so universally employed in trade and manufactures, that not only it cannot be equalled in England, but perhaps not in Europe'. The industry in these areas was on a large scale, but very dispersed as most of the work could easily be done by hand in the workers' homes with the whole family helping out. Most workers combined spinning or weaving with small-scale farming, so that they tended to live outside the towns.

Norwich, with a population of about 35,000, was the centre for an industry employing 70,000 to 80,000 people and Halifax is an even better example. The town of Halifax had a population of only 6,000 but the parish which included the workers was one of the largest in England and in 1720 it had a population of 50,000. Once again it is Defoe who gives a vivid impression of the look of the cloth industry before the Industrial Revolution: '. . . the nearer we came to Halifax,' he writes, 'we found the houses thicker, and the villages greater in every [valley] bottom; and not only so, but the sides of the hills, which were very steep every way, were spread with houses, and that very thick, for the land being divided into small enclosures, that is to say, from two acres to six or seven acres each, seldom more, every three or four pieces of land had a house belonging to it . . . hardly a house

By the late 18th century brick and tile kilns such as these near London were a common sight in the southern countries – an early sign of industrial growth. With fewer natural resources and a less concentrated urban population (apart from the capital itself), many of the worst features of northern industrial development were here averted.

standing out at a speaking distance from another, and . . . we could see at almost every house there was a tenter and on almost every tenter a piece of cloth, or kersie, . . . from which the sun glancing, and as I may say, shining (the white reflecting its rays) to us, I thought it was the most agreeable sight that ever I saw . . . look which way we would, high to the tops, and low to the bottoms, it was all the same innumerable houses and tenters, and a white piece upon every tenter.'

The Halifax weavers were unusual because they were mostly independent workers. Elsewhere the capital was provided by a clothier or cloth merchant who supplied the workers with the necessary tools, organized the supply and collection of materials, and paid them at piece-work rates as his employees. This was a well-organized capitalist industry with a kind of rural proletariat using non-industrial methods of production. No dramatic increase in production could take place until machines were invented to help each worker to produce more. However, machines of any size would need artificial power to drive them – water or steam – and their introduction would mean the end of the 'domestic' system and a change-over to factories.

It was the new cotton industry, not the older and prouder woollen industry which led the way. For centuries cotton cloth had been made exclusively in the East, and India had clothed much of Asia as well as supplying the European market through Dutch and English merchants in the 17th century. Slowly, Europeans began to use cotton themselves and by the middle of the 17th century Manchester was making cloth with cotton. At first this was coarse cloth – fustian – having a linen warp and a cotton weft, because the powerful wool interests resented the intrusion of cotton and Acts of Parliament prohibited the production of pure cotton until 1774.

The cotton industry, however, had one great advantage over wool. Because it was a new industry, it was free from the restrictions which controlled the woollen industry, and as it grew up in new, unincorporated towns like Manchester it did not have to conform to the regulations of the old town charters. Silk had similar advantages but the English climate does not suit this material and although towns like Macclesfield became noted for their silk they never developed so dramatically as cottons in Lancashire and Derbyshire. Cotton-spinning needs a fairly constant temperature and a damp atmosphere. The hills to the north and east of Manchester stop the clouds blowing in from the sea, and

rain falls quite steadily (forty inches a year), so that this and a temperature which rarely varies from between 40 °F and 60 °F makes Lancashire an ideal home for cotton.

Inventions paved the way, and the first was a simple device made by John Kay in 1733. Until then the width of cloth a man could weave alone had been limited by his arm span because he had to throw the shuttle from one hand to another. Broader cloth needed two men, one at each side of the loom. Kay's flying shuttle allowed the weaver to send the shuttle through the web by pulling a string and in this way enabled him to weave broader cloth alone. It also speeded up the weaving process so that when it came to be used widely after 1760 it greatly increased the demand for yarn. This had always been in short supply because at this stage it could only be spun in single threads on a spinning-wheel. About 1760, however, a carpenter and weaver called James Hargreaves had invented a simple machine for spinning eight threads at once, and in 1767 he produced a few for sale only to have his Blackburn home smashed up by angry workers who were sure that the invention would put them out of work. He moved to Nottingham and patented the 'Spinning Jenny' in 1770 after which it became widely used to meet the demand for yarn.

It was the work of Richard Arkwright that brought the real breakthrough. In 1769 he patented a water-frame which spun cotton by rollers and was powered by water. It is doubtful whether Arkwright could properly claim to have invented this machine because it was very similar to an invention by John Wyatt and Lewis Paul in 1738, but it is certain that Arkwright's business ambition led to the widespread use of the machine. In 1771 he joined forces with two rich hosiers, Need of Nottingham and Strutt of Derby and set up his mill at Cromford near Derby. By 1779 the Cromford mill housed several thousand spindles and employed 300 workers. This was the start of the immensely successful career of 'that bag-cheeked, pot-bellied, much enduring, much inventing barbar!', who 'gave England the power of cotton'. His water-frame, together with Richard Crompton's 'mule', invented in 1779 and so called because it was a cross between the jenny and the water-frame, having both rollers and spindles, gave Lancashire cotton thread as strong and as fine as the best Indian thread and gave it in abundance. In this way spinning became a fully fledged factory industry.

Factory weaving came more slowly. Edmund Cartwright, a

Prior to the introduction of the power-loom weaving was done at home. The high attic windows in these early 19th-century weavers' cottages at Macclesfield belong to the workshops over the living quarters.

parson, first invented a power-loom in 1785 but this model was impractical and it was not until improvements including constructing the loom of iron had been made by two Stockport men, Radcliffe and Horrocks, in 1803, that it could be used in factories. After this, it was used in ever greater numbers (see page 24) and the fate of the hand-loom weavers, the princes of the pre-industrial cloth industry, was sadly and rather violently sealed. The United States had a hand in the revolution in textiles also, because without Eli Whitney's cotton-gin (1793), which enabled the short-stapled American cotton to be separated cheaply from the seed, England would not have had the enormous supplies of American cotton on which she relied.

So it was that the remote but grimly beautiful valleys of Lancashire and Derbyshire acquired their tall millstone-grit factories with the workers' houses clustering round them. At first they were built by streams to supply the power but gradually they came to use steam, and tall chimneys began to ruin the clear air of the Pennines. Machines of iron and power by steam called for revolutions too in the harnessing of power and the production of iron. These revolutions in their turn demanded vast increases in the output of coal from the seams with which these islands are, or were, so richly blessed.

The birth of the first industrial nation

By the beginning of the 19th century, coal was Britain's main fuel; steam-engines pumped water from mines, worked bellows, drove hammers and machinery; and iron was the raw material for these machines. The marriage of coal, steam, and iron laid the foundations for Britain's role as 'Workshop of the World'.

Left: *Boiler engine invented by Richard Trevithick, one of the pioneers in the development of steam-power.* **Right:** *Early 19th-century pumping system – the first commercial use of steam in Cornish mines.*

Before the Industrial Revolution the basic raw materials of industry had been plants or animals – wood, leather, wool, flax, cotton, hemp – and energy had been supplied either by human and animal muscle-power, or by simply harnessing natural phenomena like air and water as and when they occurred. When there was no wind, the windmill could not function and, though primitive devices had enabled men to control the flow of water through water-mills, a drought would bring them to a halt. Men were still largely the prisoners of their natural environment. The large-scale use of steam, coal, and iron helped them to create their own artificial environment by using machines which did not depend on the accident of geography or climate. Of course, coal and iron had been used before the Industrial Revolution and it was to be a long time before human ingenuity processed natural resources much more fully to produce synthetic materials and atomic energy, but civilization took a new turn with the revolutionary developments in iron and steam towards the end of the 18th century.

Coal was already an old industry by 1750. It had been mined in Northumberland in Roman times, and from the 16th century onwards production had increased enormously not only in the north-east but also in small pits in the Midlands, in north and south Wales, in Scotland, and in Cumberland. As early as 1700, Britain was producing about 3,000,000 tons of coal a year, twice the amount produced by the rest of Europe. By 1750 shafts as deep as 600 feet or more were being sunk to meet increasing demands, and the industry was in the hands of big capitalists. The mining community was fully established well before the Industrial Revolution and, though mine-working was helped a

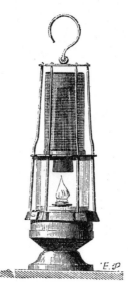

Above left: *The Watt/Boulton steam-engine from the famous Soho Works, near Birmingham. It was Watt's ingenious invention, but Boulton's capital secured the best workers, and made it a commercial proposition.* **Above right:** *The famous Davy safety lamp saved thousands of lives, and allowed work in dangerous mines.* **Opposite page:** *Part of a steam-engine at the Coalbrookdale iron works, pioneer of cast-iron production in the early 18th century. By the end of the century iron foundries were making extensive use of Boulton's and Watt's steam-engines.*

little by technological advances, the life of a miner remained basically unaltered. In this sense there was no revolution in coal, simply a vast increase in output.

Coal-miners had a reputation for brutishness. Arthur Young in 1768 called them 'a most tumultuous, sturdy set of people, greatly impatient of controul, very insolent, and much void of common industry', and they were accused of drunkenness and riotous living as soon as they had a little money in their pockets. 'It is to high wages,' wrote the Rev. Thomas Gisborne in 1798, 'that many of the criminal habits, so often ascribed to the character of a collier, may in part be ascribed', and he is appalled to see them immediately after a pay-day 'indulging themselves in the use of animal food three times a day'. It is true that in good times the wages of the miner might be twice that of the agricultural labourer, but work was not always available and it is difficult to imagine any work more dangerous or brutalizing than that of the early miner.

Each pit-head had a wooden gin over the mouth which lowered the workers (women and children as well as men) down to the coal-face in hazel-wood baskets which were also used to raise the coal. The gins were worked by horse-power and they were so cumbersome and slow that it took a team of four horses working at a fast trot two minutes to raise six hundredweight of coal 600 feet. Lighting down the mine was very poor, because until 1815 no safe and adequate lamp had been invented. Candles were impossibly dangerous at any depth and the first substitute, the steel mill, was difficult to operate and produced very little light. Until iron came to be used for props, the seams were held up by pillars of coal left by the miners as they cut into the seam, so that there was a great danger of a cave-in.

Ventilation was a great problem in deep mines; foul air would suffocate and fire-damp caused many explosions. No decent fan was invented until the middle of the 19th century, and before then the main means of ventilation was provided by a furnace which sucked cold air through the workings. The flow of air was controlled by doors which were opened and closed by little children aged six or seven who sat alone in the dark for hours on end. The other danger in deep mines was flooding, and though there were systems to lead off the water, or pumps to raise it out of the mine by animal-power, such methods could not cope with very deep workings. A mine in Warwickshire, for example, used 500 horses to raise the water by buckets. It was only when

Opposite page: *Silhouette of a pithead with its massive colliery winding machine. Prior to the invention of the steam-engine miners were lowered from the surface in horse-winched baskets and the coal hoisted up in buckets by the same method.*

efficient steam-pumps had been invented that the flood menace could be controlled.

Work in such conditions must have been a living hell. The hewn coal was put into trucks which were hauled along wooden rails by horses or boys and then loaded on to the backs of women, the load being so great that it took two men to adjust it. Weeping with the strain, the women would carry the coal up ladders sometimes for hundreds of feet until it could be put into buckets at the base of the shaft and horse-winched to the surface. Conditions were not always as bad as this, but mine work left its victims physically crippled and mentally stunted. 'Cut off from the light of heaven for sixteen or seventeen hours a day', wrote Richard Atkinson in 1765, 'they are obliged to undergo a drudgery which the veriest slave in the plantations would think intolerable, for the mighty sum of fourteenpence.'

The first recorded accident in the north-east was in 1658 as a result of flooding. The victims were not buried until 1695 when, as the parish register records, 'the bodys were found intire after they had lyen in the water thirty-six years and eleven months'. Disasters became more frequent in the 18th century as the mines went deeper. A 19th-century newspaper recalls an accident at Chatshaugh colliery on the Wear in August 1756: 'The foul air in one of the pits ignited, by which four men were instantly killed and torn to pieces. The explosion was so violent that a corf full of coals was blown up the shaft from a depth of 80 fathoms into the open air, and a vast quantity of coal dust and rubbish was thrown to a great distance. . . . The explosion was so loud as to be heard by people in their beds nearly two miles off, rumbling like thunder or the discharge of many cannon. Had it happened an hour later, the whole of the workmen would have been in the mine, consequently the destruction of human life would have been dreadful.'

The Industrial Revolution brought a little relief to miners, but this was usually a by-product of technological advances which enabled mine-owners to sink deeper shafts – down to 1,000 feet by 1830 – and so produce the quantities of coal demanded by the new industrial society. In 1815, both Sir Humphry Davy and George Stephenson produced a safety lamp which was to save thousands of lives but, as Mr Buddle, a colliery inspector, admitted, a great advantage of the 'Davy' lamp was that it allowed work in dangerous mines. 'This introduced quite a new era in coal mining,' he said, 'as many collieries are now in

existence, and old collieries have been reopened, producing the best coals, which must have lain dormant but for the introduction of the Davy lamp.' The same is true of the use of steam-pumps in mines. By 1770 there were perhaps sixty Newcomen steam-pumps at work in Northumberland, and Watt's improved pumps were being installed in the 1790s. These certainly reduced the danger of flooding and made life more tolerable for the miners, but their main purpose was to allow deeper working. Essentially, therefore, the miner's life remained what it had been. Coal was to provide more and more fuel, but by methods which remained largely unmechanized until the 20th century.

The exploitation of steam

Of all the many factors which contributed to the Industrial Revolution, the most revolutionary and the most impressive was not coal but steam-power. J. L. and Barbara Hammond said that steam-power 'declared the triumph of industry and the glory of man'. From clumsy and inefficient beginnings it was quickly improved to open up tremendous possibilities for industrial progress. The limitations of muscle-power are obvious, and though water had served well to work bellows and hammers in ironworks, or to turn machinery like the water-frame and the mule in the textile industry, it could only be applied in a limited way in Britain. For water-power is most useful in a land with many fast-flowing streams and, apart from areas like the Pennines, Scotland, and Wales, this country's rivers flow slowly. The Alpine area of Europe, and much of the United States relied on water-power for much longer than Britain, and hydro-electricity has brought water back into its own in many parts of the world. The geographical limitations of Britain's water-power, however, necessitated finding an alternative solution to the problem.

When water vaporizes it expands 1,800 times. The idea of harnessing this energy is far from new. It was probably used by Hero of Alexandria in the 1st century B.C. to open temple doors or to pour libations apparently by magic. Hero's writings were rediscovered during the Renaissance and many people, including, for example, the Marquis of Worcester (1601–67), experimented with devices using steam. Regretfully, therefore, we must dismiss the old myth that steam-power was born in the mind of a bright Scots lad called James Watt as he sat one winter's evening watching his mother's kettle boil on the hearth. Watt's contribution to steam is incalculable, but steam-pumps had been used in Britain for over seventy years before he began his work.

The first steam-engine used in industry was invented by Thomas Savery (1650–1715). Called 'The Miners' Friend or an engine to raise water by Fire', it was patented in 1698 and worked on simple principles. It pumped water from wells quite efficiently and was used successfully in Cornish copper-mines, but its limitations were revealed when it was tried in the Broadwater Collieries in Staffordshire in 1706 and was found to be capable of pumping water up no more than 100 feet. When greater pressure was used the boiler burst. Thereafter, Savery's engine was used to supply water in gentlemen's houses or to work fountains – tasks it could perform effectively, though not quite safely as there was no pressure-gauge.

It was Thomas Newcomen (1663–1729), a Dartmouth blacksmith and ironmonger, who produced the first steam-pump to be used widely in industry. It was known as an 'atmospheric engine' because, in contrast to Savery's engine, the steam in the cylinder was not used to drive the pump but only to create a partial vacuum when condensed. Ordinary air pressure drove the piston into the cylinder and this raised the pump which was connected to the piston by a see-sawing cross-beam. A large piston meant that it was possible to gain more force without increasing steam pressure and this made Newcomen's engine much more powerful than Savery's.

The first engine was made about 1706 but it was a clumsy affair. The piston did not fit tightly into the cylinder and condensation, which was achieved by pouring cold water on the outside of the cylinder, was far from complete. Moreover, the tap controlling the passage of steam into the cylinder was worked by hand seven or eight times a minute. These difficulties were ironed out by 1720; water was now sprayed into the cylinder to improve condensation, the operation of the taps had been made automatic, and a safety-valve had been fitted to eliminate the danger of explosion.

The improved engine soon became standard equipment in most large mines, and it was also used to pump water into canals and to supply drinking-water in towns. It is difficult to know exactly how many were in use by the second half of the 18th century but in 1767 fifty-seven were found around Newcastle, and there were eighteen in Cornish mines in 1780. Though they

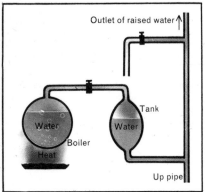

Thomas Savery's Engine 1698

The water in the boiler is heated to make steam, which passes, when the valve is opened, into the tank. The tank is then doused with water from a pipe above, and the steam condenses, creating a partial vacuum. Thus, water is drawn up the up pipe, and forced out.

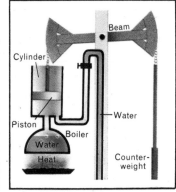

Newcomen's Engine 1706

Water is heated in the boiler to make steam, which passes into the cylinder and forces the piston up, assisted by the counter weight. Water is then admitted into the cylinder. The steam condenses and creates a partial vacuum, thus drawing the piston back down again. A see-saw motion is set up which is used to drive a pump.

A painting (detail) of one of the largest and most successful ironworks in the country at Cyfartha. Iron extraction was a complex chemical process – and expensive, but new developments meant that more iron could be produced more cheaply.

had obvious advantages and the purchase price was not very great, there was sales resistance at first, largely because they were very expensive to run. 'The vast consumption of fuel in these engines is an immense drawback on the profit of our mines', wrote an owner in 1778, 'for every engine of magnitude consumes £3,000 worth of coals per annum. This heavy tax amounts almost to a prohibition.' This was certainly a deterrent to all but coal-owners, but pumps at mines could burn low-grade slack which could hardly be sold elsewhere, and this made them relatively cheap to run. Mines remained loyal to the Newcomen engine well into the 19th century, mainly because they were cheap to buy and performed their simple task effectively, but they were very inefficient pieces of engineering as 80 per cent of the energy produced was wasted.

It was left to a man of truly outstanding ability to make steam-engines really efficient and to extend their use from simple pumps to almost every industrial process. James Watt was far more than a clever inventor and his achievements are in a completely different class from those of most of the leaders of the Industrial Revolution. His grandfather was a teacher of mathematics and his father was a skilled architect and shipbuilder who also served as Treasurer of Greenock and a local magistrate. James was born in 1736, a sickly boy who suffered from headaches for most of his life, and the only survivor in his family; two brothers and a sister died in infancy and his other brother was drowned at sea.

James soon showed his mechanical abilities and at the age of thirteen he was making models in his father's workshop. In 1755 he spent a year in London learning how to make mathematical instruments, having to do this secretly and to stay indoors most of the time because he was defying the laws of apprenticeship by rushing through his study in one year instead of the customary seven. When he returned to Glasgow in 1756 he was barred from setting up as an instrument-maker in the town because he was not officially qualified and it was only because the University authorities gave him refuge within the University that he was able to work at all. This was a lucky chance because it brought him into contact with leading scientists, including Dr Black, the Professor of Chemistry.

In Glasgow he developed his scientific interests, teaching himself French, Italian, and German in order to be able to read foreign scientific works, and he made experiments to improve the barometer and the hygrometer. To eke out his income, for

Use of Boulton and Watt Steam Engines 1775-1800

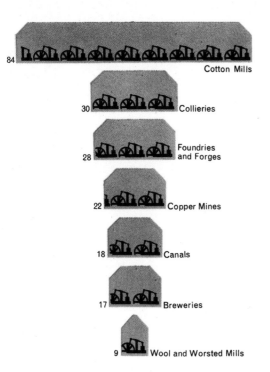

84 Cotton Mills

30 Collieries

28 Foundries and Forges

22 Copper Mines

18 Canals

17 Breweries

9 Wool and Worsted Mills

the demand for mathematical instruments in Glasgow was not great, he turned to repairing musical instruments and through this he became a passionate lover of music. He had an insatiable curiosity and a passion for knowledge of all sorts. 'I saw a workman and expected no more; I found a philosopher', said his friend Robison when he first met him in 1758.

It was in the winter of 1763–4 that the University sent Watt a small Newcomen engine for repair and this led him to carry out a series of experiments to eliminate its deficiencies. The two main weaknesses which Watt saw were that the cooling system did not provide sufficient condensation, and a great deal of fuel was wasted after each piston stroke in raising the temperature in the cylinder. Watt tells how he was walking in Glasgow one Sunday afternoon in 1765 when 'my thoughts turning naturally to the experiments I had been engaged in for saving heat in the cylinder, the idea occurred to me that, as steam was an elastic vapour, it would expand, and rush into a previously exhausted space; and that if I were to produce a vacuum in a *separate* vessel, and open a communication between this and the steam in the cylinder, such would be the result'. (My italics.) Like most great ideas, it was very simple. Two different temperatures were needed and it made more sense to have these in two separate containers than to waste fuel changing from one to the other in a single container. In his early experiments, Watt not only introduced this separate condenser but also fitted an air-tight cover on the cylinder so that the piston was pushed down by pressure of steam instead of air. This transformed Newcomen's 'atmospheric engine' into a genuine steam-engine.

It was one thing to make a working model, quite another to make it a commercial proposition. Watt had very little money and it was necessary to find a backer who was willing to speculate in a machine which had not been proved to work in a large size. Machine-making was not very precise at this time and it was not at all certain that parts could be made with sufficient accuracy to meet the requirements of Watt's design.

His first patron was Dr Roebuck who owned the Carron Ironworks in Scotland. Dr Black introduced Watt to Roebuck who was immediately interested and pressed Watt to pursue his invention. The prospect of contact with big business worried Watt, who was a poor businessman, and he delayed seeing Roebuck for three years. Even when they went into partnership in 1767 Watt dallied so annoyingly that Roebuck wrote to him: 'You are

English and Welsh Coalfields c. 1830

NORTHUMBERLAND AND DURHAM

WHITEHAVEN

YORKSHIRE, NOTTINGHAMSHIRE AND DERBYSHIRE

LANCASHIRE

NORTH WALES

NORTH STAFFS

SHROPSHIRE

DUDLEY AND WARWICKSHIRE

FOREST OF DEAN

SOUTH WALES

BRISTOL

SOMERSET

Cort and iron puddling

now letting the most active part of your life insensibly glide away. A day, a moment, ought not to be lost.' Roebuck needed Watt's engine to pump his water-logged mines. Eventually, a patent was taken out in 1769 but the prototype was a failure; faulty workmanship let him down. Discouraged, Watt shelved the project. 'Of all things in life,' he said 'there is nothing more foolish than inventing', and when, in 1772, Roebuck went bankrupt, hopes of success seemed to be at an end. It was his great good fortune that as part of what was owed to him by Roebuck, Matthew Boulton took over a two-thirds share in Watt's invention. So began one of the great partnerships of the Industrial Revolution.

Boulton was an outstanding manufacturer who owned the famous Soho Works two miles north of Birmingham, which had an international market and numbered among its customers Catherine the Great of Russia. The works was powered ineffectively by water, and Boulton was well aware of the great advantages of Watt's machine, if only it could be made to work commercially. But, as he wrote, 'The thing is now a shadow; 'tis merely ideal and will cost time and money to realize it.' Both were provided. Watt's patent was extended by twenty-four years in 1775 and Boulton's capital bought the best workmanship, so that two successful engines were made in 1776, one for the blast-furnace of John Wilkinson, whose skill had made an efficient cylinder.

Orders now came from the Midlands and the scepticism of London was overcome by a successful demonstration at the Bow Distillery. As the market opened up, most orders came from Cornwall, and by 1780 forty engines had been sold to the Cornish mines. But success did not bring wealth, because Boulton and Watt were not paid directly but by a system of royalties, and the Cornish mine-owners, who had already paid the supplier for the engine, were loath to continue paying. Boulton suffered financially and Watt suffered in health and morale, yet it was at this dark period that Watt made his most revolutionary breakthrough, rotary action.

The leap forward

So far, steam had only been used for pumping. Textile factories using new machinery had to be placed near streams to provide power, but if steam could only be made to turn the machinery then the possibilities for expansion would be boundless. Characteristically, Watt was pessimistic but Boulton had no

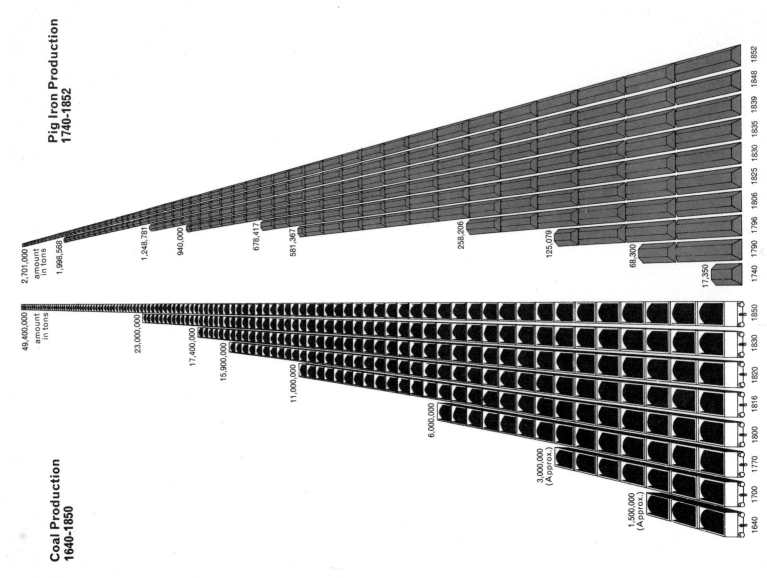

Pig Iron Production 1740-1852

amount in tons

2,701,000 — 1852
1,998,568 — 1848
1,248,781 — 1839
940,000 — 1835
678,417 — 1830
581,367 — 1825
258,206 — 1806
125,079 — 1796
68,300 — 1790
17,350 — 1740

Coal Production 1640-1850

amount in tons

49,400,000 — 1850
23,000,000 — 1830
17,400,000 — 1820
15,900,000 — 1816
11,000,000 — 1800
6,000,000 — 1770
3,000,000 (Approx.) — 1700
1,500,000 (Approx.) — 1640

Contrary to popular belief, Watt was not the pioneer of steam-power as such — its use probably dates back over a thousand years previously — but he did invent the modern condensing steam-engine. Thus his first steam-engine did in fact revolutionize the use of steam-power.

doubts and with his encouragement Watt was able to patent a device in 1781 which worked by the so-called 'sun and planets' system. This worked by a small cogwheel, attached to a shaft connected to the beam, coming into contact with a much larger wheel which was thus set into motion. Boulton's hopes were justified and orders for the new machine increased steadily after 1785. Industrial centres became 'steam-mill mad' and a foreign visitor to Swansea in 1802 was amazed at the number of engines in use: 'some are used for pumping water out of mines, others for hauling up the coal, and others still for moving, grinding and rolling mills'. By 1800, steam-power working to Watt's principles, had come into its own (see left). Before long it had ousted all other sources of power and become the motive force behind the first industrial nation. Watt died wealthy in 1819, having spent his last years in cultured retirement, giving little encouragement to plans to extend the use of steam-power. Obviously machines would need to be sturdy to withstand this new steam-power. And it soon became obvious that machines made of wood were quite inadequate for the job. Manufacturers, therefore, began to turn towards machines made of iron, and between 1750 and 1835, iron output increased fifteenfold.

'About five miles from Newcastle', wrote Arthur Young in 1768, 'are the iron-works, late Crawley's, supposed to be among the greatest manufactories of the kind in Europe. Several hundred hands are employed in it, insomuch that £20,000 a year is paid in wages. . . . The quantity of iron they work up is very great, employing three ships to the Baltic, that each make ten voyages yearly, and bring seventy tons at a time, which amount to twenty-one hundred tons, besides five hundred tons more freighted in others. They use a good deal of American iron, which is as good as any Swedish, and for some purposes much better. They would use more of it if larger quantities were to be had, but they cannot get it.' These ironworks produced anchors, hoes, spades, hooks, chains, and so forth, and Newcastle was also famous for cutlery 'after the manner of Sheffield'. Sheffield itself was the centre of a thriving industry and it rivalled Birmingham as the leading iron-manufacturing area in the country. Birmingham specialized in ironmongers and toys.

Evidently iron manufacture was thriving, and in fact England was using twice as much iron *per capita* annually as France, but, as Arthur Young pointed out, most of the iron used was imported. This put great limits on the industry which was at the mercy of

The cast-iron bridge over the Severn, first of its kind, was built in 1779. Iron became the raw material for the building of the 'first industrial nation'.

Working in a living hell; coal-mining was a dangerous and brutalizing life. Conditions were appaling: foul air caused suffocation, fire-damp caused explosions, and there was the ever-present danger of flooding. This Victorian engraving shows a miner 'holing' bottom coal.

foreign suppliers. Imported iron was bound to be more expensive than British, and international tension or war could cut off supplies altogether. The situation was all the more frustrating because British iron production had increased steadily in the 16th and 17th centuries.

The old home of iron production had been the Sussex Weald which Camden had noted in 1607 'is full of mines everywhere, for the casting of which there are furnaces up and down the country [i.e. county], and abundance of wood is yearly spent. Many streams of water are drawn into one channel, and a great deal of meadow ground is turned into pools for the driving of mills . . . which, beating with hammers upon the iron, fill the neighbourhood day and night with their noise'. By the 18th century, however, the iron industry was declining and, though Defoe remarked on the extent of the Sussex industry in 1724, by 1740 there were only about sixty furnaces working in the whole country. Production was 17,000 tons, so that each furnace yielded only 300 tons a year. This output was enough for only a third of the iron needed even at this stage and it was only a tiny fraction

A miner travelling along a low tunnel.

of that needed for an industrial society. (See chart of iron production on page 42.)

The decline resulted from a serious shortage of wood which was turned into charcoal for the blast-furnaces. This shortage could not be overcome by a straight switch to coal because the reduction of iron-ore is an extremely complex chemical process. The iron can be ruined by vegetable or mineral impurities in the furnace, and even when the metal has been successfully extracted its quality is determined by subtle differences in the mix in the furnace. This makes iron extraction an art rather like Cordon Bleu cookery, and it was a very long time before coked coal could be made to serve as an adequate substitute for charcoal. Success was eventually achieved by many small, unrecorded modifications, and though a few individuals made important contributions, it is really a story of continuous development.

The Quaker, Abraham Darby, was the first man to use coke successfully in a blast-furnace. As early as 1709 his furnace in Coalbrookdale was being fed by a particularly good type of coke, but in the early years his iron could only be used for cast-iron goods and it was not until 1750 that his son, also called Abraham, discovered a mix that produced iron good enough to be made into bar-iron at forges. The Darbys' methods were not widely adopted, however, and in 1762 the Society for the Encouragement of Arts, Manufactures, and Commerce was offering prizes for iron which could be made as well with coke as with charcoal. None the less, the Darbys prospered and their cast iron was used in great quantities to cast pots, fire-backs, boilers, and water-pipes. The first iron rails for wagon-ways were cast at Coalbrookdale in 1767 and the first cast-iron bridge was erected over the Severn in 1779. Gas lighting, which was introduced at the beginning of the 19th century, also used cast iron for pipes. (The tremendous increase in pig-iron production in the period can be seen in the chart on page 42.)

However, cast iron is brittle and there was a great need for cheap and improved methods of converting cast iron into wrought iron which will take stress. From the 1730s, many experiments were made to use coal rather than wood to make wrought iron. These usually used a refinery hearth and often a reverberatory fire where flames did not play directly on the metal, but in 1784 Henry Cort, a contractor to the Navy, and Peter Onions, a foreman in an iron-mill at Merthyr Tydfil, both developed a new method known as 'puddling', within a few

The Nant-y-glo ironworks in South Wales, as it was in 1780. The new processes of puddling and rolling were by now revolutionizing the industry. Coal and iron transformed the nation's economy but helped to destroy the rural atmosphere of the British landscape.

months of each other. Pig-iron was put into a reverberatory furnace, fed by coal, and in the door of the furnace were holes through which bars were pushed to stir the metal. The *Annals of Agriculture* describes the process: 'When melted, [the iron] spits out in blue sparks the sulphur which is mixed with it. The workman keeps constantly stirring it about, which helps to disengage the sulphurous particles; and when thus disengaged, they burn away in blue sparks. In about an hour after melting, the spitting of these blue sparks begins to abate (the workmen stirring all the time), and the melted metal begins to curdle, and to lose its fusibility, just like solder when it begins to set.'

By Cort's method the clotted iron was then reheated, hammered

During the 17th century, horse-drawn wagons running on wooden rails were in common use for carrying coal from British collieries to the ports. The first locomotives were designed for colliery transport work.

into slabs, then heated once more and passed under rollers which squeezed out further impurities. This combination of puddling and rolling transformed the iron industry in England. Fifteen times as much bar-iron could now be produced as the old methods would have yielded in the same time, the new iron was better in quality, and coal was used in the process. It was suitable for all purposes, except the production of steel, but though Benjamin Huntsman developed crucible steel as early as 1740 it was not used by the Sheffield cutlers, and the great age of steel had to wait upon Henry Bessemer in the next century.

These developments in iron, taken with those in coal and steam, form a part of the story of the Industrial Revolution which runs parallel to the revolution in textiles. At first, textiles led the way, and south Lancashire was the first home of the new industrial society, but the marriage of coal, steam, and iron eventually had far wider effects and opened up Scotland, Tyneside, the Black Country, and Wales. Most of the old iron areas faded away as large-scale production gravitated to the major coalfields. The industrial processes grew together, as Arthur Young remarked in 1768: 'Rotherham is famous for its iron works, of which it contains one very large one, belonging to Mr. Walker, and one or two smaller. Near the town are two collieries, out of which the iron ore is dug, as well as the coals to work it w   , these collieries and works employ together near 500 hands. The ore is here worked into metal and then into bar iron, and the bars sent to Sheffield to be worked, and to all parts of the country; this is one branch of their business. Another is the foundery, in which they run the ore into metal pigs, and then cast it into all sorts of boilers, pans, ploughshares, etc., etc.'

By the beginning of the 19th century coal, steam, and iron were indispensable to one another. Coal was the universal fuel; steam pumped mines, worked bellows, drove hammers, and turned rolling-mills; and iron was the raw material for most of the machinery. The basic industries could thus make more, more cheaply, and so inject new life into all other branches of industry, especially textiles. Improved transport cheapened and speeded the flow of goods so that the economy was able to expand as never before, and by the time that Queen Victoria came to the throne the 'first industrial nation' had been born. It was a painful birth, and, though industrialization has now brought untold benefits to mankind, the early years meant exploitation and misery to the first victims of a new order.

Stupendous achievement, appalling suffering

The railway engine revolutionized transport and helped to speed industrial growth.
North and south were linked for the first time but the filth, disease and overcrowding
in the northern factory towns was a running sore for which there seemed no cure.

*An engine at Coalbrookdale – the 'new monster' that was to cause
'the most complete disturbance of quiet and comfort' in the country.
In spite of angry opposition, the railways developed rapidly – their
speed and the volume of traffic they could carry made them
irresistible.*

Most of the radical changes which made the Industrial Revolution had come about by 1830 but a very important feature of the first industrial society had hardly shown itself by then. Canals had made it possible to transport heavy goods all over the country but barges were very slow-moving and by the middle of the 19th century they had largely been ousted by railways. Rails of wood, later lined with iron, had been used in the 18th century to move coal and iron to the coast or to a canal. At first the heavy loads had been carried in huge wagons drawn by teams of horses but by the end of the century engineers were trying to make a 'travelling engine' using steam-power. Richard Trevithick, a Cornishman, built the first engine to run on rails in 1804 and it was used in a South Wales ironworks. An improved version, the 'Puffing Billy' (now in the Science Museum in London), was built for the coal-mine at Wylam in Northumberland and was able to carry twenty tons at 5 m.p.h.

However, it was not until 1825 that the first public railway, between Stockton and Darlington, was opened to move coal from Durham. George Stephenson, who was brought up at Wylam and whose father was a fireman on a colliery engine, was responsible for the construction of this first line. Like so many of the early engineers, Stephenson had to struggle for his education. For years he attended evening classes after long hours of colliery work, devoting his hard-won savings to becoming an engineer. After the success of the Stockton–Darlington Railway, Stephenson was appointed in 1826 to build a projected line linking Manchester and Liverpool. This was completed in 1830 and Stephenson had the satisfaction of seeing his locomotive, the 'Rocket', outclass its rivals in a competition to decide which

Left: *George Stephenson's 'Rocket', one of the first and most famous locomotives. The 'Rocket' won the competition organized by the Liverpool and Manchester Railway in 1829, pulling a 20-ton train at an average speed of fifteen miles per hour. With its multiple boiler, the 'Rocket' incorporated the basic features to be used in all later steam locomotives.*

Below: *This watercolour by Rowlandson shows one of the first steam trains on a demonstration track near Euston Square, London. It was built in the early nineteenth century by Richard Trevithick.*

engine should be adopted for the new line.

Thereafter railways developed very rapidly. In 1833 the Leicester–Swannington line (built to transport coal) began the Midland system and in 1838 both the London–Bath–Bristol and the London–Birmingham lines were opened. By this time a total of 500 miles of railway were working. The country was fascinated by this wonderful new form of transport – passenger traffic at first was more important than freight – and a powerful 'railway party' in Parliament, headed by George Hudson, the 'Railway King', encouraged a mania of investment so that by 1850 no less than 6,084 miles of track were open. Despite a financial crisis in 1847 when thousands of small investors were ruined and Hudson was discredited, the railways continued to expand and by the outbreak of the First World War 20,000 miles of track existed. By 1850 more money was being made from freight than from passengers and the worst fears of the canal-owners and turnpike trustees had been realized.

Just as canals had had to meet opposition from vested interests, so railways were attacked by pressure groups which used all manner of emotional arguments against the new monster. Speeches in Parliament at the time read like those against the development of air space today. 'What was to be done', it was said, 'with all those who have advanced money in making and repairing turnpike roads? What was to become of the coach-makers and harness-makers, coach-masters, coachmen, inn-keepers, horse-breeders, and horse-dealers? The beauty and comfort of country gentlemen's estates would be destroyed by it. Was the House aware of the smoke and the noise, the hiss and the whirl which locomotive engines, passing at a rate of ten or twelve miles and hour, would occasion? Neither the cattle ploughing in the fields nor those grazing in the meadows could behold them without dismay. Lease-holders and tenants, agriculturists, graziers, and dairy-men would all be in arms. . . . It would be the greatest nuisance, the most complete disturbance of quiet and comfort in all parts of the kingdom, that the ingenuity of man could invent.' Such arguments rarely prevail against economic interests, and the speed of railways and the volume of traffic they could carry made them irresistible. Railways took over the service that canals had so successfully begun.

At the same time the protesters had a case, and it was not just the railways that caused the 'complete disturbance of quiet and comfort'. The destruction of 'the beauty and comfort of country

An engine coupling at Coalbrookdale. By mid-century 'Railway Mania' had led to the indiscriminate laying of lengths of track throughout Britain. By 1850 there were over 6,000 miles of railroads, and both private and public opposition gradually subsided.

gentlemen's estates' was one of the lesser evils brought on by the Industrial Revolution. At first the countryside was hardly affected and until 1850 the majority of the population still lived in the country. But from the start those who were directly caught up in the process of industrialization were beset by all manner of social problems which men have been trying to solve ever since. The economic advances were bound to bring radical changes to the structure of society but no one was able to anticipate what those changes might be and plan accordingly. In social terms, therefore, Britain stumbled into the Industrial Age with its eyes shut.

Slums, poverty and disease

There was no doubt that the growing towns in the north of England would soon have to suffer the consequences of unplanned expansion on the cheap. Of course, filth and disease were rampant in rural England but overcrowding made conditions intolerable and as early as 1755, when it was only beginning to expand, Manchester was seen to be very sordid by John Clayton in his *Friendly advice to the Poor*. 'A general nastiness', he wrote, 'is become even a public scandal to our town. We cannot walk the streets without being annoyed with such filth as is a public nuisance . . . We are grown infamous for a general want of good manners in our populace . . . Our streets are no better than a common dunghill, and most sacred places are most shamefully polluted . . . Our very churchyards are profaned with such filth as were intended to create a detestation and abhorrence even of idol temples. I mean they are rendered no better than errant draught houses.'

Forty years later John Aikin wrote his famous *Description of the Country from thirty to forty Miles around Manchester* in which he claimed that Manchester was suffering from all the troubles of London, only more intensely: '. . . the poor are crowded in offensive, dark, damp, and incommodious habitations, a too fertile source of disease! . . . In some parts of the town, cellars are so damp as to be unfit for habitations . . . The poor often suffer from the shattered state of cellar windows. This is a trifling circumstance in appearance, but the consequences to the inhabitants are of the most serious kind. Fevers are among the most usual effects; and I have often known consumptions which could be traced to this cause. Inveterate rheumatic complaints, which disable the sufferer from every kind of employment,

An 1830 caricature by John Leech showing Hyde Park as he imagined it might be when railway engines finally replaced horses. Ironically, it was to be another, free-ranging wheeled monster, the motor car, which would later pollute the air and shatter the peace of town and country alike.

are often produced in the same manner . . . I have often observed, that fevers prevail most in houses exposed to the effluvia of dunghills in such situations.'

Perhaps the worst conditions were in the lodging-houses where men coming to the town to find work in the mills had first to live. The houses simply could not cope with the demand for beds. 'The lodging-houses', wrote Aikin, 'produce many fevers, not only by want of cleanliness and air, but by receiving the most offensive objects into beds, which never seem to undergo any attempt towards cleansing them from their first purchase until they rot under their tenants . . . The horror of these houses cannot be easily described; a lodger fresh from the

HYDE PARK AS IT WILL BE

The dinner-hour in Wigan. Factory girls gather for lunch and gossip at the town pump — a haven amidst the grim and filthy 'palaces of industry'. Though toiling at least ten hours a day, factory workers were allowed hardly any time for eating and recreation.

country often lies down in a bed filled with infection from the last tenant, or from which the corpse of a victim to fever has only been removed a few hours before.'

Manchester was not noticeably worse than other new towns. In 1845 the crowded courts and alleys of Nottingham were horrifying. 'They are noisome, narrow, unprovided with adequate means for the removal of refuse, ill-ventilated, and wretched in the extreme, with a gutter, or surface-drain, running down the centre; they have no back yards, and the privies are common to the whole court: altogether they present

The Industrial Revolution created new social and political issues, widening the gap between owner-manager and workers. The bitter conflict of interests fostered socialist theories and experiments and led to the formation of the first trade unions.

scenes of a deplorable character, and of surpassing filth and discomfort. . . . In these confined quarters, too, the refuse is allowed to accumulate until, by its mass and its advanced putrefaction, it shall have acquired value as manure; and thus is sold and carted away to the "muck majors", as the collectors of manure are called in Nottingham.'

Crowded like penned cattle in houses built as cheaply as possible, sometimes with walls only half a brick thick, deprived of light, beset by vermin and the all-pervading stench of human effluvia, the working class of the early industrial towns lived lives of utter degradation.

Water was a particular problem. Tolerably efficient systems piped water to the end of each row of houses or into each courtyard but the water was only turned on for limited periods, sometimes on only two days in the week. The inefficiency of this system is revealed by evidence given in 1840 to the Select Committee on the Health of Towns: 'There is one circumstance which very much affects the atmosphere in those districts [in Liverpool] in which the cellars are particularly [*sic*]; there is a great deal of broken ground, in which there are pits; the water accumulates in those pits, and of course at the fall of the year there is a good deal of water in them, in which there have been thrown dead dogs and cats, and a great many offensive articles. This water is nevertheless used for culinary purposes. I could not believe this at first. I thought it was used only for washing, but I found that it was used by the poorer inhabitants for culinary purposes. . . . There is a good supply of water for the poor, if they had the means of preserving it. The water is turned on a certain number of hours during the day, four hours, perhaps; the poor go to the tap for it; it is constantly running; and each person fetches as much as they have pans to receive; but they are not well supplied with these articles, and in consequence they are frequently out of water. It is not sufficient for washing, or anything of that kind.' Small wonder that there were cholera epidemics in 1831–2 and 1848–9.

The situation got out of hand largely because it developed so quickly. The population of the industrial towns rocketed and existing local authorities were quite inadequate to cope. There were many examples of local initiative – in 1796 a Board of Health was set up in Manchester – but they were never able to keep pace with the problem. It needed the pioneering research work of men like Dr Kay (later Kay-Shuttleworth), Southwood Smith, and Edwin Chadwick in the 1830s and 1840s to awaken the conscience of the ruling élite and to force the Government to recognize that it was responsible for the health of the population. The Public Health Act of 1848 was the first step towards national control of the problem but its provisions were largely permissive and it was left to later developments, culminating in the great Public Health Act of 1875, to come to terms properly with the problems of controlling an industrial environment.

The new towns had come into existence because of the development of the factory system, and one of the most difficult problems for the workers was how to adjust to the brutalizing nature of factory work. Work in the domestic system had been hard and the rewards had not been great riches, but at least the workers had the illusion of personal freedom. Within certain limits they could order their own lives. In the factory they were no more than expendable cogs in a machine which never stopped day or night.

In 1833 P. Gaskell described the effects of factory life on the workers. 'Any man who has stood at twelve o'clock at the single narrow doorway, which serves as the place of exit for the hands employed in the great cotton-mills, must acknowledge that an uglier set of men and women, of boys and girls, take them in a mass, it would be impossible to congregate in a smaller compass. Their complexion is sallow and pallid – with a peculiar flatness of feature, caused by the want of a proper quantity of adipose substance to cushion out their cheeks. Their stature low. . . . Their limbs slender, and playing badly and ungracefully. A very general bowing of the legs. Great numbers of girls and women walking lamely or awkwardly, with raised chests and spinal flexures. Nearly all have flat feet. . . . Hair thin and straight – many of the men having but little beard, and that in patches of a few hairs, much resembling its growth among the red men of America. A spiritless and dejected air, a sprawling and wide action of the legs, and an appearance, taken as a whole, giving the world but "little assurance of a man", or if so "most sadly cheated of his fair proportions".' Such were the effects of working twelve hours or more a day, six days a week, in a temperature of 80°F, with doors and windows tight shut to maintain the necessary humidity, under the eye of a stern and sometimes vicious overseer who maintained a rigid code of discipline. The factory bell became the most hated symbol of the new order.

Much of the suffering in the early factories could hardly have

In the northern cities, where industrialization was more rapid, living conditions were far worse than elsewhere. The task of providing new houses for the working population was first tackled— but only on a local, voluntary basis—by the Artisans' Dwelling Act of 1875. Subsequent legislation was unable to keep pace with population growth and the problem — typified by these closely-crammed workers' houses in Salford—still remains a century later.

Factory conditions were often appalling. This late Victorian picture shows a girl combing wool, stripped to the waist because of the suffocating heat. Only gradually, with the passage of successive Factory Acts — the first effective in 1833 — were the worst abuses rectified, but long hours and low wages prevailed throughout the century.

been avoided. The owners of small mills were working to narrow profit margins so that they could not afford more than the most rudimentary working conditions. They had no understanding of the psychology of labour and so it is not surprising that they took the simple view that the number of hours worked was directly proportional to output. Reduction of the working day, it was argued, would inevitably lead to bankruptcy. There were many cases of thoughtless exploitation and wanton cruelty, until gradually the consciences of humane men were awakened.

At first it was only the plight of children in factories which drew the attention of reformers. Because the early textile-mills were water-powered they had to be situated near fast streams, often in sparsely populated areas. The problem of finding labour was solved by the so-called 'apprenticeship' system. Pauper children were sent from all over the country by local Poor Law authorities who made contracts with the mill-owners to maintain supplies. There was no outside control of conditions and the children were used as entirely expendable labour. If some died of disease or brutal treatment they could easily be replaced by parishes usually only too glad to be relieved of the burden of keeping the children. Despite an Act of 1802 to regulate conditions for the apprentices, the system continued because of the lack of proper inspection, until the coming of steam-power made it unnecessary to place mills away from centres of population. Henceforth, the children of adult workers would work as 'free labourers' unprotected by the Act of 1802.

Nothing effective was done until the Ten Hour Movement developed in the 1830s. This was sparked off by a blistering attack on child labour by Richard Oastler which appeared in the *Leeds Mercury* on 16 October 1830. The letter read: 'Thousands of little children, both male and female, *but principally female*, from seven to fourteen years of age, are daily *compelled* to *labour* from six o'clock in the morning to seven in the evening, with only – Britons, blush while you read it! – *with only thirty minutes allowed for eating and recreation.* Poor infants! ye are indeed sacrificed at the shrine of avarice, *without even the solace of negro slaves*; ye are no more than he is, *free agents*; ye are compelled to work as long as the *necessity* of your needy parents may require, or the cold-blooded avarice of your worse than barbarian master *may demand!* Ye live in the boasted land of freedom and *feel* and mourn that *ye are slaves*, and slaves without the only comfort that a negro has. He knows that it is his sordid, mercenary master's

58

interest that he should *live*, be *strong* and *healthy*. Not so with you. Ye are doomed to labour from morning to night for one who cares not how soon your weak and tender frames are stretched to breaking!'

Two years later a Parliamentary Select Committee was set up under the Tory Evangelical, Michael Sadler, to look into child labour and, though the Committee's report was clearly propagandist, its grim picture was largely corroborated by a Royal Commission in the following year and the first effective Act controlling hours and conditions for children was passed.

Sadler's report told some dreadful stories. Elizabeth Bentley, whose job was to take bobbins off the spinning-machine, was permanently crippled at the age of twenty-three by years of long labour. Samuel Coulson's two young daughters had been forced to work nineteen hours a day for six weeks when the mill was busy. They had had to get up at 2 a.m. after only four hours' sleep and at the end of the day were frequently too tired to eat. The eldest girl's forefinger was screwed off at the knuckle when her nail was caught in the machinery, for which she not only received no compensation but had her wages stopped for the five weeks she had to spend in Leeds Infirmary. Reports of beatings and long hours were repeated time and again.

However, the report of 1833 made it clear that the worst conditions existed in the smaller, older mills. They were 'dirty, low-roofed; ill-ventilated; ill-drained; no conveniences for washing or dressing; no contrivances for carrying off dust and other effluvia; machinery not boxed in; passages so narrow that they can hardly be defined; some of the flats so low that it is scarcely possible to stand upright in the centre of the rooms.' All these evils were being eradicated in new mills and there is no doubt that many improvements came naturally with greater prosperity. However, the work of the Ten Hour Movement was invaluable, and its efforts led to women's hours being regulated by an Act of 1844 and men's hours by 1850. The mass of laws controlling hours and conditions of work today stem from this final realization by the Government that industrial society has to be regulated.

Membership certificate of the Cotton Spinners' Union. The Combination Acts, finally repealed in 1824, had outlawed unions, which were regarded by the Government as hotbeds of revolution.

Although local authorities did their best to combat the social evils caused by industrialization, legislated reform was not adequate to cope with the terrifyingly high incidence of poverty, disease and crime which disfigured Victorian society. Conditions in some areas were so frightful that children such as these were forced to scavenge in pig troughs to keep themselves alive.

The workers organize themselves

Could the workers, then, do nothing to help themselves? They tried, but by 1835 it seemed that they had failed. The handloom-weavers suffered greatly when machinery began to deprive them of their livelihood. In the 18th century they had been the most prosperous of textile workers. William Radcliffe looked back on the 'Golden Age' of the 1790s with perhaps exaggerated enthusiasm: 'Their dwellings and small gardens clean and neat, – all the family well clad, – the men with each a watch in his pocket, and the women dressed in their own fancy, . . . every house furnished with a clock in elegant mahogany or fancy case, – handsome tea services in Staffordshire ware, with silver or plated sugar-tongs and spoons.' With wages of about twenty-five shillings a week such modest comfort was quite possible.

Within a decade, however, wages had dropped to about thirteen shillings, and by 1818 the handloom-weavers were reduced to starvation level on wages of about eight shillings. The stocking-frame knitters of Leicester and Nottingham suffered a similar decline. From the prosperity of the 18th century when 'each had a garden, a barrel of home-brewed ale, a week-day suit of clothes and one for Sundays, and plenty of leisure', they had found their livelihood destroyed by the use of wide-frame looms from which low-quality 'cut-up' stockings were made. Both the handloom-weavers and the stocking-frame knitters blamed new techniques and machines for their sudden penury. Unrest and riots became more frequent until they reached their peak in 1811–12 with the Luddite movement. This was simple direct action in which workers tried to stop industrial advance by breaking up machines. It is not known whether their supposed leader, Ned Ludd of Sherwood Forest, actually existed but they must have been well organized because they were able to defy troops of soldiers for a long period. A thousand wide-frames were destroyed in Nottinghamshire, power-looms were broken in Lancashire, and in Yorkshire a heavy hammer named 'Great Enoch' was used to smash up the shearing-machines which put the croppers out of work:

> Great Enoch still shall lead the van,
> Stop him who dare! Stop him who can!

Eventually, after murders by both workers and mill-owners, the uprisings were put down. Government spies and *agents provocateurs* uncovered many of the ringleaders, who were hanged or transported. Luddism had its martyrs but no lasting success.

Less violent movements were no more effective in the first half of the 19th century. While the Government had no objection to Friendly Societies, which existed among the better-off workers purely for welfare purposes, it was rigidly opposed to combinations of workers to press for better wages or conditions. Such organizations smacked of revolution, and with France torn apart by revolution at the time the British Cabinet saw its primary duty to be preventing the evil from spreading across the Channel. The Combination Acts of 1799 and 1800 outlawed unions and it was not until 1824 that they were repealed, but even then the unions' powers were very uncertain.

The early unions were astoundingly ambitious. John Doherty was mainly responsible for the creation of two national unions – The Grand General Union of all the Operative Spinners in the United Kingdom (1829) and the National Association for

An early trade union procession. It was the skilled, better-paid artisans who first joined together in their mutual interests, but before 1850 unions were organized on a sectional and local basis. Thereafter, the 'new model' unions were national in scope, restricting membership to legally apprenticed workmen. Less skilled workers had to wait till the 1870's for representation. The Trades Union Congress was founded in Manchester in 1868 and three years later the movement was given legal section.

The development of commercially practical steam engines transformed human society. The brighter side of this transformation is shown in this picture, as the elegant steamship Britannia *here sets out on her maiden voyage from Liverpool in the year 1840.*

the Protection of Labour (1830) – but despite resolutions proclaiming universal solidarity they had both collapsed by 1832. The leaders lacked experience, the unions had no funds, and members could hardly be expected to strike when to do so would at the very least mean that their jobs would be filled by people out of work. Nevertheless, idealism continued to flourish and early unionism reached its peak in February 1834, with the formation of Robert Owen's Grand National Consolidated Trades Union. Owen was an extremely successful and humane mill-owner and a romantic Socialist. The aim of his union was nothing less than the end of the capitalist system. Each trade or craft was 'to constitute one grand company or association, comprising all the individuals in the business throughout Great Britain and Ireland; but each trade and manufacture to be united to all others by a general bond of interest by which they will exchange their productions with each other upon a principle of equitable exchange of labour for a fair equal value of labour'. A rule book was drawn up and within a few weeks the G.N.C.T.U. claimed a membership of 500,000.

Most of the members, however, were unskilled and the leaders were divided over the best method of attack. The Government was worried by the danger of widespread strikes and acted firmly. Unions could not be prosecuted simply for attempting to press for better wages or shorter hours, but industrial action such as strikes might be interpreted as 'obstruction' or 'intimidation' and be punished accordingly. Six agricultural labourers from Tolpuddle were made the unfortunate victims. They were accused of taking unlawful oaths and after a trial which had obviously been prejudged they were sentenced to seven years' transportation. George Loveless and the other 'Tolpuddle Martyrs', decent simple workmen with no thoughts of revolution, became the first heroes of the Trade Union movement, but their trial marked the end of the first phase of unionism. It is now clear that the unions are a necessary part of an industrial society but it was not until the 1850s, after years of quiet consolidation, that the second phase – New Model Unionism – began to enjoy some success among skilled trades, and only in 1906 were unions made safe from legal prosecution.

It took a long time for society to begin to cope with the problems created by the Industrial Revolution. Considering the suffering and class hatred that it caused at first, it is not surprising that Marx and Engels predicted that the first proletarian

Industrialization led to overcrowded, unhygienic living conditions in cities. Some authorities, inspired by men such as Edwin Chadwick, did their best to tackle what was virtually an insoluble problem and the passage of the 1848 Public Health Act had a limited alleviating effect. Rebuilding London's archaic sewer system was one unpleasant but vital task in improving the health of the capital's teeming population.

revolution would be in England. It was avoided by a combination of good luck, rapidly increasing prosperity, and intelligent pragmatic government. By 1867 most town workers had gained the right to vote and so became part of the political nation. By 1870 a national system of education had been initiated, inadequate at first but maturing slowly into something valuable for the individual, and indispensable for a technological age. By the beginning of the 20th century the first steps were being taken to convert curative social legislation of the 19th century into something more creative – the Welfare State.

The financial demands of modern society are enormous and can only be met because of the rapid development of the economy since 1800. Production, in general, increased at a faster rate in the seventy years after 1830 than in the period of the Revolution itself. Ten times as much coal was produced in 1900 as in 1830, and more than twelve times as much iron. Cotton could hardly be expected to maintain its amazing rate of growth between 1760 and 1830, mainly because at first only tiny amounts of imported cotton had been used. Nevertheless, imports of raw cotton rose by 600 per cent between 1830 and 1900, and the value of British exports as a whole rose by 800 per cent in the same period. These figures may give the impression that the period of the Industrial Revolution was not after all particularly remarkable. If there are such dramatic developments in the second half of the 19th century why has so much attention been devoted to the earlier period? The point is that before the Revolution the economy had never expanded at a rate fast enough to change its nature. Between 1760 and 1830 for the first time it began to expand at a rate of 2 per cent a year, twice the previous rate and enough to allow what is called 'the take-off into sustained economic growth'. This growth rate continued throughout the 19th century, reaching a peak of $2\frac{1}{2}$ per cent between 1875 and 1895, and made Britain for a time the 'workshop of the world'. But by then other countries had reached the point of take-off.

Seen in retrospect, the techniques and inventions which helped to bring about the Industrial Revolution may seem crude or even quaint and a 2 per cent rate of growth is small compared, for example, to the 9 per cent which Japan has already achieved in this century, but they were enough to transform the world. It is this which makes the Industrial Revolution one of the most important events in the history of mankind.

Index